DEDIC.

This book is dedicated to the memory of my lifelong companion and loving wife, Patricia.

ACKNOWLEDGMENTS

I want to thank the many people who have sent me letters, talked to me on the radio, and met me at personal appearances, who helped make this book possible. You have helped me to better understand money and how to accumulate it, and also how thousands of you feel about money. I also want to thank the people who helped me write this book. On college financial aid, Phyllis Wordhouse, Plymouth, Michigan; on life insurance, Robert P. O'Leary, Choice-Quote, Menlo Park, California; and on estate planning, attorney M. Franklin Parrish, Walnut Creek, California.

I am also grateful to Cynthia Zigmund, my editor at Dearborn Publishing; to my own editor, Dan Bickley, who read and edited my manuscripts and labored desperately at times to keep the subject within the grasp of every reader; and to my son Richard and my daughter Nancy, who helped me remember what I had told them over the years.

But most of all, I want to thank God for the strength to see this book through after the sudden death of my loving wife. All of my previous six books have been dedicated to her, my lifelong companion. Before her death, she encouraged me to pull together what I have learned in personal finance and share it with my readers. I have left the references to her in the book, just as I had written them, as this is what she would have wanted. I know that I still love her very much, and I hope and pray that this is the book she would have wanted.

CONTENTS

INTRODUCTION

What are the most important things I've learned in life—things I've done each day that have put me on easy street as I head toward retirement? Things that I talked about over and over with my kids as they were growing up, until one day my wife said, "Why don't you write those things down in a book?"

This book began when I realized that over the years, the little things that I did each day turned out eventually to be the big things in building my wealth. So for my son and daughter, I wrote down a few words of instruction and reflections on my life that I hoped they would keep in mind as they married and built their own lives.

The stories you are about to read teach a simple lesson: If you follow a few basic rules, you can avoid most money problems later on in life. You may not agree with all the conclusions that I've drawn from my life's experiences, and obviously some are more important than others, but as my son told me, "Dad, the simple steps I now take each day have let me forget about money problems. Now I'm adding my own experiences and someday I'll give them to my two sons."

When *my* father spoke to me about money, he usually began the conversation by saying, "Have I said that if you don't get your financial habits in order early in your life, you won't have time later on?" Millions of Americans apparently never talked to my dad. According to a 1996 survey by TransAmerica Occidental Life Insurance Company, 63 percent of Americans worry about having enough money to pay their monthly bills, and 69 percent worry that they won't be able to retire in the same style as their working years.

It used to be that we learned what we needed to know from our teachers in school and from our life experiences. In my own case, looking back over 30 years of professional financial planning, I can say with certainty that no one I met on Wall Street or in the media has had a more lasting effect on my life than the savvy farmers I knew in my youth. Their secret? They used time and savings to get rich. In fact, even before I went to the university to study money management, I learned all I really needed to know about making money from talking with farmers.

Over the years, I've also talked with some remarkable people on Wall Street and in the media. Many of them are famous and their advice is featured on television and in financial magazines. They tell other people what to do with their money, yet most of the time, they fail to beat the average guy who just invests in the entire stock market and then goes off to play golf.

I've also learned that authors can attract a lot of attention if they make dire predictions of the stock market's coming meltdown or a depression just around the corner. None of these authors has been right in the past, but their market-bashing, survivalist themes have helped them sell a lot of books to people who either want to get rich quick in a roaring bull market or bury gold coins in the backyard to use as money of last resort.

In the media we are presented with an overwhelming and frequently contradictory mass of information, which (we are told) we must understand if we are to keep up with the times. But most of us read this mass of computer-generated information without comprehending it, see it without learning how to use it, and hear it without understanding its ramifications. In reality, there are ever-widening gaps between what we understand and what we think we understand, and also between what we really *need* to understand and what we're told by the media we *should* understand.

As the "teacher" in this book, I'm not going to give you any pie-in-the-sky or doom-and-gloom stories. I'm just going to tell you what has worked for me over the years. Because I'm also the messenger, I get to choose which messages I deliver. And the fact is, despite the billions of bits of raw information spilling out of the media, flowing over the Internet, and appearing in ads from your bank or broker, most of what you read and hear about what to do with your money is nothing more than hype dressed up to look different from an old story you've heard many times before.

This book is drawn from the experiences and reflections of my life. I've learned that many people I talk with live their lives backwards. They want to earn more and buy more so they'll be happy. But first they need to determine what they really want in their lives and for their family in order to have those important things later on in life.

This book is also about my belief over the years in making and keeping money the old-fashioned way and about learning the time-tested basic rules of investing. I've learned that all of us have a choice every day regarding our attitude for that day. We cannot change our past. We cannot change the inevitable. The only thing we can do is rely on what we have—our attitude. I'm convinced that life is 10 percent what happens to us and 90 percent how we react to it.

This book is also a collection of lessons that tell a simple tale: Becoming wealthy today is very easy . . . but it's also very boring. When I was young, everything was possible and it seemed as if I could always make more money the day after tomorrow. Today, I know my life is graying when I get junk mail from people telling me it's almost too late to get a pension or that I need to exercise at least 30 minutes a day if I want to see my next birthday. Time catches up suddenly to us all. But I've found, as I head for retirement, that over the years a few simple changes in my lifestyle have made the difference between a retirement filled with European vacations and one spent working behind a fast-food counter.

I've also learned that the most important things you can do in life are to make yourself happy, to share your love and understanding with your family, and to take each day one day at a time. After all, your trip to financial success should be as much fun as arriving at the destination.

Read a lesson each day and talk about it with your family and friends, add your own observations, and find out if it works for you as it has for me.

—Jim Jorgensen

Growing Up

My mother always told me that when I met someone I should introduce myself right away. And when I meet people I usually follow my mother's advice. However, my mother also told me that proper folks don't talk about themselves. But, as a reader, I think you are entitled to know something about me.

I need to start off by telling you I don't know everything— I only know what's worked (and what hasn't) for me over the past 40 years. Not only do I not know everything, my family tells me I can't cook, I can't buy the right clothes, I can't remember birthdays, and I continually talk about my youth. But a wise man once said, "If you want to know how you feel about something, remember your youth." So let me tell you a little about mine.

Until I was 11 years old, I lived in what to me was a big city—Omaha, Nebraska. Then my family moved to a small farming community in central California. Over those years, our household would today be called "economically disadvantaged." I didn't know that at the time, but I did know, since my family didn't own a car, that if I wanted to go someplace, I had to walk. If I wanted extra spending money, I had to work. And when I went to a birthday party, I had to bring a gift. My mom usually bought the gift, but then one day she gave me $2 to buy one. "What can I buy?" I asked. She said, "Buy whatever you'd like, I'm sure Johnny will like it, too." So I went to the store and found just what I'd always wanted. But I had to work on my mom to let me keep the gift. I tried the ploy that Johnny might not like it and maybe we should get another gift. Mom didn't buy that. Then I said it had batteries and maybe we should break the package to see if they were any good. Mom said we'd trust the batteries. I even tried to get sick the day of the birthday party in the hope that mom would forget about the gift. Do you know what it's like to give to someone else a birthday gift that you've always wanted? That's the whole deal with birthday parties, except I never forgot that day and I vowed that someday I'd have enough money to buy the things I wanted.

When I got to high school, I had two summer jobs that kept me from having empty pockets the rest of the year. But they were also the kind of jobs that made you want to get out of town and go to college so you could make enough money to escape cleaning canal banks and unloading cantaloupes all your life.

I also got a clothing allowance. To save money, I wore a T-shirt and a pair of jeans. My dad sided with me, but my mother did not share my idea of how a well-dressed high school student should look.

"But Mom . . . all the guys wear just a T-shirt and a pair of jeans," I said. As usual, my mother was wrong and totally unreasonable. Just ask any teenager; they know how "out of it" their moms can be. But my mother was right about one thing—how to save money. She had saved enough money to buy an evaporated water cooler attached to one bedroom window. Of course, it was my parents' bedroom window.

Later on, when my wife and I moved to the big city, my two kids wanted cars in high school, the boy to chase after girls and the girl to drive to school. Remembering that my dad didn't own a car until I was a senior in high school, I told them there was no way they could get wheels. I later sent them both to college, but they still didn't own a car.

Now, as I ponder the past, I know I've had a happy life. I've been married for more than 40 years and I have two children who are married and starting their own families. But the past is very different from the present: my son has five cars and my wife and I have just two.

LESSON 2

It Can Happen to You

After 24 years of hard work with Magic Industries, you find an envelope on your desk. You're already working overtime for no extra pay and your once-generous health insurance plan has been switched to an HMO that puts your doctor in another town. You rip open the envelope and discover you are roadkill in the company's plans to downsize. One more confused employee smack in the path of management's plans to boost profits and sell the company at a humongous profit.

You think this might be a good time to head for the mountains and open a bed and breakfast and say goodbye to Magic Industries. Then you remember that your pay hasn't increased much over the years, and you also haven't noticed where you've put your savings.

What I'm about to tell you may not make you a millionaire, and it won't help people who wake up late in life and discover they haven't watched where they've saved their money, but if you still have time to save, it could give you a better lifestyle in retirement than you ever dreamed possible.

I was doing a weekend financial planning seminar when I met Mary Thompson, whose story touched me deeply. She told me that she had worked hard her entire life, and the success she had dreamed of had turned into failure.

"You know," she told me, "I'm about to retire and I now find I have to keep working just to survive and pay my house and car payments. About 30 years ago I started taking my savings to a bank because a friend I trusted worked at the bank and he told me my money would be safe. What he didn't tell me was that the 3 percent my money was earning would never amount to much. Now, Mr. Jorgensen, this shoe box of money isn't looking very good. I have to continue to work because I don't have enough money to retire."

I felt the pain in Mary's eyes and I asked her why she continued to stash her savings in the bank.

"I just didn't know," she said, "and now they tell me I can't even collect all my Social Security benefits because I have to continue to work."

Mary is a little wiser now. The trouble is, I can't come up with something that can go back in time and allow her to start over. If Mary had put $5,000 into a savings account 30 years ago and it had paid 5 percent a year, she would have accumulated about $21,500 today. But if she had invested the same amount of money in a stock mutual fund earning 12 percent a year, she'd now have about $150,000. Drawing from her 5 percent savings account she'd now get about $90 a month, but from the money in the stock fund, about $625 monthly.

What's even more impressive is if Mary had put $2,000 a year into good stock funds earning 12 percent a year, after 30 years, ignoring taxes, she might have $540,000. Earning 5 percent now on this nest egg, she'd have a *monthly* income of $2,250.

In college I learned a few things, but most of what I found helpful later on came from talking with the teachers after class. One thing I clearly remember occurred on a rainy day when most of the students had already left the classroom. "Son," the teacher said in a way that was sure to get my attention, "it makes no difference what you earn over your life, but it makes a big difference what you do with your money."

LESSON 3
Sleight of Hand, Loss of Pension

*"Like a magician's vanishing act, a good
part of your pension can disappear
even before you collect it."*

Everybody loves a magic show. First you see something, then you don't. Magicians create the illusion that what we thought we saw was real. But recently on my radio show, a guest who was both a stockbroker and a magician told me that it's really all in the hands. Not that you need to be a magician to be a stockbroker, he said, but it never hurt. He put an ad in the classified section of the local newspaper that had my name and the three of hearts. Then, on the air, he had me draw a card from the deck and it was the three of hearts. He then showed me the ad in that day's paper. To this day I still don't how he did it, but his sleight of hand was perfect.

Maybe, like millions of other Americans today, you live in terror of a poverty-stricken old age lost in a blizzard of credit card bills. But, you tell yourself, you've been working for the company for many years and you can, at least, rely on a good company pension.

Now, what I'm about to tell you may seem like it's from a magic act, but it's real. Most likely, that pension you are expecting has an "integration" section in the plan. Integration provisions were put in most pension plans years ago to save employers money. Their justification was that the company was only promising a certain level of income in retirement, and the pension was to be part of it. Therefore, most pension plans today have a 50 percent "integration" level. Like a magician's vanishing act, part of your pension can disappear even before you collect it.

"They lied to me about my pension," a man about to retire told me. "I'll get a lot less than I expected. They promised me $25,000 a year, but since I will collect about $12,000 a year in Social Security benefits, they want to cut my pension about $6,000 a year. What do you think, Mr. Jorgensen? Is this fair?"

"It may not be fair," I said, "but this is the way most company pensions work."

So we began a long conversation about how pensions work, but we always came back to the integration section of the plan. Unfortunately, most people don't discover this section of their retirement plan until they are near retirement or about to collect their first pension check. What they find, in plain English, is that if they receive other benefits, such as Social Security, then these benefits can be used to reduce the company's pension payout. With a 50 percent integration level, half of most additional benefits the worker collects can be subtracted from the company's pension check. I know this may sound a bit absurd and weird, but believe me: this is how most company pensions work.

And the day is not far off when younger workers will have to wait beyond age 65 to collect their full pensions. That's because there is a growing trend to link today's age 65 company pension benefits to the same age as full Social Security benefits. Those affected could be those born after 1937, with the age of eligibility for full pensions rising each year. For example, under this plan, those born in 1943 or later would collect the highest company pensions and Social Security benefits at age 66; those born in 1960 or later at age 67.

Now I don't want to throw a bucket of cold water on your expectation of a hefty pension, but if you think you'll reap a windfall when you retire, you'd better first read the fine print. The point of this lesson is that your retirement planning can have a happy ending if you learn the basics of your pension plan and rely on yourself to take care of yourself later on. The government won't do it, your kids won't, your company—if you're lucky to stay with it long enough—won't, and that leaves only *you*.

LESSON 4
Everyone Can Do Something
Using $2.74 a Day to Build Wealth

I know from my own life, and from talking to people all across America, that ordinary people can accumulate extraordinary amounts of money if they follow a few basic rules and save a few dollars each month from their paycheck.

The most compelling reason for building a retirement nest egg yourself is that today employers call all the shots.

Company pensions are fast disappearing, and with massive corporate downsizing, job security has evaporated, leaving most people feeling like a yo-yo tossed between one paycheck and the next. Worse yet, employers use temporary workers to plug any gaps and they turn the job spigot on when business picks up and off when business cools.

Now, how about some good news for a change? Something to make you feel better after you've been blown out of a job after 20 years with a company. Yes, you can take care of yourself without any help from anyone else—all you need is yourself.

When I say this at my Saturday financial seminars, there is always someone in the audience who looks at me with suspicion. But I've discovered over the years that what you make at work does not control what you can accumulate for your retirement. What's important to understand is that building wealth depends more on changing your spending habits than on the size of your paycheck.

If you're a 20-something, the cost of financial security starting now will be tiny, but even if you're a middle-ager facing a late-life financial security crisis, the cost can be well within your reach. Taking it one day at a time, even if you only save $2.74 a day, $1,000 a year, and you invest in stock mutual funds, you could have the money you'll need to get by in retirement.

How do I know this will work? Because both *Time* and *USA Today* says it has worked, and it has worked for me. Over the past ten years, the stock market, as measured by the Standard & Poor's 500 stock index, had an average annual total return of about 15.3 percent. *USA Today* (January

17, 1997) said that if you invested $10,000 on December 31, 1986, you would have $41,935 on December 31, 1996. *Time* magazine (January 27, 1997) reported the same numbers and said that over the past ten years the S&P 500 stock index rose 314 percent.

If the stock market continues to make the same average gains over the next ten years, you'd double your money every five years. A single $2,000 investment in good stock funds in an individual retirement account could be worth $8,000 in ten years, and $32,000 in 20 years.

You can figure how long it will take to double your money by using the "Rule of 72." Just divide 72 by the annual rate of return you expect to receive. A 15 percent return will double in 4.8 years, and double again after 9.6 years. A 4 percent fixed saving rate will double in 18 years, and double again after 36 years.

The point in this lesson is that to turbocharge your investment returns, you need to understand the correlation between the performance of stocks and fixed savings. The mere act of saving money is not enough. Investing without taking a risk is not enough. What's important is to overcome your fear of losing even one cent of your savings. When people believe they are taking no risk, they are, in fact, taking a big risk on rising inflation and the loss of their money's purchasing power in the years to come. But probably the biggest risk of all is simply doing nothing with your money. The mattress may be a safe place for money, but it can kill your future retirement nest egg.

If you intend to build real wealth, you must consider the amount you expect to earn on your money each year. Let's say you invest $1,000 a year and go long-term in stocks. Between 1986 and 1995, the Standard & Poor's 500 stock index had an average annual return of 15.2 percent. That same $1,000 a year in short-term U.S. Treasury bills had an annual return of 5.55 percent. To make it simple, let's call the annual stock return 15 percent and the Treasury return 6 percent. At the end of just ten years, the total in your nest egg of stocks could be $23,000, in Treasuries just $14,000. But over a 20-year period, the value of the stocks could be $118,000, and the Treasuries only about $39,000.

My dad, who worked through the Depression as an accountant, knew how to make every penny count. Back then, when passbook savings were paying about 2 percent, he told me the only way to make money double was to hold a dollar bill up to a mirror and look at it. He may have been right in the 1930s, but over the years on Wall Street the numbers have changed. A letter from a reader of my newspaper column tells the story.

"My 23-year-old daughter recently started working. She is making payments into her stock mutual fund from her paycheck each month until she reaches $10,000. Thereafter, she doesn't want to invest in the market anymore. She wants to leave the $10,000 in the mutual fund and let it mature until retirement."

If the record of Wall Street for the past 15 years continues, and she leaves the money alone, she could have about $1 million at age 65. No promises, no guarantees, but even with inflation, her retirement nest egg should enable her to retire in comfort without ever investing another dime. That's the kind of fairy tale you can believe in.

I know that many of you are saying that mutual funds don't love you anymore. A lot of funds now kick out investors with small balances, and the minimum to open an account with many funds is $2,500. After a recent seminar, when most of the folks had left, Tom came up to me and said, "Mr. Jorgensen, what you say about building wealth is fine, but I just don't have the money to start." With an embarrassed look on his face, he asked me, "Why don't you ever tell people how to start building wealth on a shoestring?"

"Tom," I said, "can you afford $25 to open a mutual fund account and $25 a month automatically from your checking account?"

His eyes lit up. "Now," he said, "you're talking my kind of language."

I told him about several stock mutual funds that allow you to start with a minimum investment of $25, and thereafter at least $25 a month drawn automatically from your checking account. You can find these mutual funds by talking to a financial planner or by calling the funds you see in the magazines or newspapers.

Despite the fact that our public schools rarely teach about personal finance and investing, there *are* ways parents (and grandparents) can help kids learn about money, save for college, and even begin to build a large retirement nest egg. Several mutual funds help kids learn about money, but Stein Roe & Farnham's Young Investor Fund is leading the way in helping kids of junior- and senior-high-school age learn about money.

The cornerstone of its efforts is a growth stock mutual fund with investments in McDonald's, Disney, Nike, Coca-

Cola, Toys "R" Us, and other companies kids see everyday. The average shareholder is nine years old, and 85 percent of shareholders invest every month using dollar cost averaging. During a recent radio program I talked with Katie, a 14-year-old investor from Illinois, who said, "Every morning I grab the stock pages to see how my fund is doing. My mom thinks it's great and she can't believe the money I'm making." Another investor in the fund, Chris, a 12-year-old from Massachusetts, told the audience, "I first had my money in a bank account and I didn't make much money, so my mom and dad said to invest in mutual funds. So far I've made $400. It's much better than having my money in a piggy bank."

To help kids who invest in the fund learn more about money, Stein Roe has a great package of learning tools. A quarterly newsletter, *Dollar Digest,* is written for young investors and it includes quizzes, crossword puzzles, stories about the stocks in the fund, and information regarding what other kids are doing to learn about money. There's also an activity book, *You and Your Money,* written for younger kids. It's a coloring, puzzle, and learning book. Lastly, there's *The Young Investor Game,* an easy-to-operate interactive computer game for kids. Players learn about risk, income taxes, financial planning, mutual funds, Wall Street, and money in a fun, graphical setting.

Sometimes kids have all the luck. The Stein Roe & Farnham Young Investor Fund was started in 1996, and in its first year it returned a whopping 35 percent, almost twice the total return of the average general stock mutual fund. There are no guarantees that any stock mutual fund will continue to turn in the same high-powered performance, but based on past history anyone at any age with a regular monthly investment plan can still build wealth and at any age, it can be done on a tight budget.

The point of this lesson is that nothing much has changed in the game of building wealth. No matter how early in your life you start to invest, no matter how much money you earn, if you make regular investments, you should build wealth the same way I did when I started on Wall Street.

LESSON 5
Make Your Own Way
Credit Card Catastrophe

"Hooked on plastic, people continue to transfer their future wealth to their creditors."

It's said that if you put a frog in boiling water, it will jump out. If, on the other hand, you put the frog in cool water and gradually increase the heat to boiling, the frog will ignore the rising temperature and die.

People, it turns out, often act like a frog. Most people would never think of jumping into boiling water by purchasing a car with a credit card, but months of easy spending can cause the water to boil as they run up against their credit limit.

A lady I know runs a gift shop. She says she can spot the easy spenders as soon as they enter her store. "They are eager to find just the right gift and they never leave the store empty-handed. But with these big-spenders, using cash is almost a lost art. With a personal check, they need two IDs and have to wait until we approve their check. Most shoppers," she says, "use a credit card and quickly take a loan against their future paycheck. I love it. They buy more when they don't have to pay for it now."

You have to take your hat off to the banks. They have figured out a way to slap on fees when you put your money in, when you keep it in the bank, and when you spend it. The newest idea is a combination ATM and debit card that works like cash. You can withdraw cash from an automatic teller machine or use the debit card and make withdrawals directly from your checking or savings account. With the debit card, the banks get a hefty fee (typically 1 to 2 percent of the purchase price) from the merchant every time you use it, and they sock you a monthly service fee to keep the card in your purse or wallet.

Debit cards also come with some big risks. Debit cards are like checks; the bank zaps your checking account instantly for the amount of the purchase. Unless you keep close track of your checking account balance, you can end up bouncing checks all over town. And it's easy to get ripped off if someone steals your debit card because there is nothing between the thief and your checking account. The person who has your debit card can clean out your bank account before you even know it. If you report the loss within two days of discovering that the card is missing, your loss is limited to $50.

But if you don't notice the loss right away, you can get stuck with $500 and you may have to fight with your bank to re-cover your money and spend lots of time straightening out your credit mess.

You also lose two other advantages when you use a debit card. First, you lose the 25-day float you have with a credit card to pay your monthly statement. With a debit card, the money for each purchase is deducted immediately. And sec-ond, you also lose the option of withholding payment for a purchase that turns out to be defective, or the opportunity to use your leverage in case of disputed charges.

In my own case, I'm the type of guy banks love to hate. I spend cash or use a credit card and pay off the balance in full each month. I avoid all bank charges and interest costs and I make the bankers pay me.

At one of my seminars, a young man said to me, "You know, I'd like to invest for my retirement but my credit card balance is up to the max each month and I'm paying over 18 percent interest. I got into trouble before I knew it. How do I get out of this mess?"

His story reminds me of the people who keep telling themselves they'll spend less than they earn and pay off their credit card balance every month. But, like some "junkie" hooked on plastic, they continue to transfer their future wealth to their creditors. The latest report I read said that 70 percent of cardholders don't pay off their balance in full each month, carrying an average balance on four to six cards of $3,800 with an average interest rate of about 18 percent.

The rule of thumb to remember when you use a credit card and don't pay off the balance in full each month is this: If the purchase price is $100, the cost to purchase this item and use a revolving balance credit card over time can be as much as $150. You're simply giving half again or more of your hard-earned money back to the bank.

You know that's true and so do I. But what happens when you don't pay off your credit card balance in full each month within the grace period? Most credit card issuers will charge you interest for the entire previous month's balance ignoring what you've already paid, and then charge you interest on your next month's statement from the date of your purchase! Some card issuers, using the two-cycle balance method, can even charge you interest *twice* on the same debt. If your monthly payment is late two or three times (and sometimes only once), the card issuer can hike the interest rate as high as 21 percent to 25 percent. At those rates, it's difficult to pay down the revolving monthly balance and get out of debt. I'm not trying to be funny. This is how credit cards really work.

If you think your state's consumer laws will help you, forget about it. The credit card issuers found a new friend who now allows them to charge higher fees on top of sky-high interest rates. In 1996, the U.S. Supreme Court ruled that if a bank bases its card operations in, say, South Dakota or Delaware, it can charge whatever late fees (and other fees) that state allows, no matter what laws are on the books where the shopper lives.

It should come as no surprise to anyone that credit card companies don't make a profit on what you buy; they make a profit on what you don't pay back each month. Credit card companies borrow money at 6 percent and charge cardholders 18 to 21 percent, so your carrying a monthly balance makes them exceedingly happy.

What does paying these high interest rates do to your financial future? Like a herd of overweight elephants stomping through a muddy riverbank, you are pounding the life out of your financial health. Let's say you run up a $2,000 balance on your credit card. Now let's say you decide just to send in the minimum monthly payment and not charge on the card again until you pay off the balance. To keep you hooked on the high-interest treadmill, the minimum monthly payment on most cards is now only 2 percent of the balance each month, or in this case, $40. That's a measly $2 for every $100 you owe. With this level of repayment, at the end of one year, your $2,000 balance will be reduced by just $100. You are spinning your wheels because virtually all the money you pay goes for interest.

Why am I telling you this? Because if you don't make any more charges on your credit card and continue to send in the minimum payment each month, you'll be paying off the original $2,000 debt for the next 33 years! You'll make the bankers happy but you'll die poor.

You don't have to fry your brain with mathematical formulas to realize that interest charges can kill. But when you pay more than the minimum monthly payment on your credit card balance, the magic begins. Mark Eisenson, in his book *The Banker's Secret,* says "The lower the required monthly payment, the greater the debt will be. "For example," he notes, "say you are carrying the typical $3,800 credit card balance at the typical 17 percent rate. You could, with no new purchases, be paying anywhere from $3,200 to $8,390 in interest by the time you pay off the debt, depending on the percent of the balance you send in every month." Eisenson points out that every extra dollar you can scrape up to help pay off your card balance more quickly will bring big rewards. For example, if you send in the minimum 2 percent ($76) monthly payment and make no new purchases, your interest totals $8,390 after 36 years and 3 months. But if you pay 3 percent of the balance (only $38 more, which is $114 per month), your total interest cost falls to only $3,222 after 16 years and 6 months.

Decide now how much you can afford to pay each month, and pay that amount every month. After you've paid off one card, take the same money and apply it to the other cards. When I realized how much of my money was going up in flames, I visualized the bank manager who issued the credit card standing there holding the matchbook and gasoline can and grinning.

A line that divides what we *can* do and what we *actually* do runs down the middle of us all. Instead of ballooning your credit card debt, you could save some money each month and pay off the balance and then put away that money for your future. By saving the interest on the typical $3,800 monthly balance at 18 percent, you'd have $684 a year to invest in a good stock mutual fund.

I know a guy who was a failure at nearly everything he tried to do. He couldn't make it as a salesman, he lost his job in his company's office, and finally he spent his remaining years at any job he could find. But even on his meager earnings, after he paid his current bills and credit cards, he never failed to save some money each day and he ultimately retired with well over a million dollars.

We all have the power to change our lives and make the most of what we earn on this earth. By simply paying off that credit card debt and investing the $684 a year in a stock mutual fund, in 20 years, with an annual total return of 12 percent, you could have about $55,000 toward your retirement nest egg.

No matter how old you are, it's still true: When you go out in the world, it's better to make your own way than ride on someone else's train.

LESSON 6
Two-Handed Cookies
Staying Invested at All Times

I don't need radar to find the kitchen when my wife is baking cookies. Just a whiff from the oven is enough. My favorite is almond twist. The recipe includes almond paste, orange rinds, and orange juice. If you've ever tasted almond twists, you know that you need one right now, but I'm always told to keep my hands off the cookies until they cool. When they are still hot, you have to shift the cookie from hand to hand. They are what I call "two-handed" cookies. Anyone can eat cold, one-handed cookies, but the temptation to eat two-handed cookies is too great for me to resist.

This seems like a good time to talk about a widely held belief: that you have to actively manage your investments to make money. The truth is that those who invest and do nothing are the big winners. Like keeping your hands off the cookies until they are cold, keeping you hands off your investments is one of the most difficult things for most people to do. Why? Because it runs counter to our drive to do something, to make things happen. Guilt and a sense of obligation are often attached to that pot of gold they are accumulating, and that makes many people feel they have to find something new and exciting to do with their growing treasure.

When we are young, we associate age with a lack of change. Even at age 30, we joke about the latest smart moves that break the mold. If we are lucky enough to reach middle age, however, we finally begin to understand that to do something just for the sake of change is not always a smart play.

To paraphrase the words of the old television show *Mission Impossible,* "Your job, if you choose to accept this assignment, is to leave your hands off your investments, ignore what you read in the papers or see on television, forget about an occasional stock market crash, and go relax." That advice has worked out well for me. I travel and take vacations. When I'm away, I can't mess up my investments by trying to outguess the market or pick a hot new stock.

"You can't believe how jittery we are," began a letter I received. "We just invested our IRA in stock mutual funds and then the next month the stock market fell and we lost a couple of hundred dollars in a week's time. We plan to invest the balance of our long-term money in mutual funds, but that dip in the market made us N E R V O U S. Why the heck don't they teach this stuff in high school? Managing your money is one of the most important things in life." My advice to these folks and others who are new stock market investors, and accustomed to having their savings locked up in insured certificates of deposit over the years, your *Mission Impossible* is to sit on your hands when the stock market takes a tumble.

Tom Henry, a broker with Smith Barney in San Francisco, told my radio listeners that "People are their own worst enemy. They look at a short-term market fluctuation like we had in July 1996 and they think that proves, shall we say, that the world can come to an end. That's like saying a rainy day just proves that agriculture can't work. You have to take a longer view.

"If you take the infinite viewpoint, which I recommend, just buying and never planning on selling, you should do very well. Hopefully I'm trying to reach the people who haven't yet made the move into the stock market. Over the last two years, the stock market has been unusual and we've come about 35 percent last year (1995) and about 26 percent this year (1996), and depending on the asset class, people have increased their net worth 60 percent by staying in the market for just this short period. But a market downturn will come, and that's the time to keep your investments in place like you were wearing lead shoes."

The most famous buy-and-hold investor is probably Warren Buffett. Buffett says he doesn't look at the stock market and interest rates don't influence his thinking. In making investments, he looks only at the stock and the company he is considering. Buffett runs the Berkshire Hathaway Corporation (traded on the New York Stock Exchange), which has large holdings in more than a dozen blue chip companies including Coca-Cola, USA Today Gannett, Disney-Capital Cities/ABC, Gillette, Wells Fargo Bank, and the *Washington Post*. Buffett seldom sells his investments and always reinvests his dividends. Had you bought Berkshire Hathaway stock at the start of 1994, your gain for the year would have been an impressive 43 percent, while most stock mutual funds broke even at best. Over the past five years ended December 31, 1995, Berkshire delivered a return of 381 percent, compared with 115 percent for the Standard & Poor's 500 stock index.

A Wall Street poster I hang over my desk illustrates why people lose their shirts: because they can't sit tight. It has a picture of a guy in a tight pair of underwear constantly moving but going nowhere.

I learned this stuff the hard way. I want you to learn before you get burned. The simple lesson is this: All the books and magazines that tell you which stocks to buy, the multitude of market-timing newsletters that tell you when to buy or sell, or your broker's advice on "hot" stocks will almost always underperform a "standpatter" who stays fully invested in good-quality stock funds and continues to save and invest. If you are paying attention to this, you'll see that becoming wealthy today is very easy, but it's very boring.

There Are No Winners
Frauds and Scams

Several years ago, my wife and I moved to New York City. We moved across the country from California because I was offered a job as a weekday talk-show host on what many consider the number one talk radio station in America, WOR-AM. This was heady stuff for a guy who worked weekends on a San Francisco radio station, and I learned quickly that what mattered most in New York City was money. Lots of money.

As we looked around New York for a place to live, I soon discovered that even with my hefty paycheck, we didn't have enough of the green stuff to live on the upper East Side, so we moved into a new apartment block on East 32nd Street. I selected the 12th floor because every floor thereafter increased my monthly rent. I also selected the 12th floor because I was told that bugs and flies could not fly higher than about the 10th floor.

I soon discovered that I had been misled when flies began resting on my windowsill and stared at me through the windowpane. Then, in their effort to fly through the glass, they hit the windowpane, fell back stunned to the sill, and lay there determined to try again. The message of this lesson is that, for flies and for human beings as well, you won't have success in building wealth if your reach exceeds what is reasonably proper to expect.

It also turned out that very little of what I was told about living in New York City turned out to be true—except, of course, that gobs of money could always bring you a better life, a larger apartment on the 30th floor, and flies on the windowsill still banging their heads against the glass.

So it came as no surprise when I read in the paper that a socially prominent, highly respected fund-raiser for the Boy Scouts and the American Cancer Society was alleged to have run a "Ponzi" scheme for several years. According to the papers, the man and his wife enjoyed the best New York could offer: a brownstone, chauffeured rides to the theater, designer clothes, and rooms full of art and antiques.

The federal fraud indictment sketches a classic Ponzi scheme in which investors are led to believe they will get rich without risk. And, like all Ponzi schemes, a few investors did pocket big returns for a while. But the promises they and others received were, in the words of federal fraud prosecutors, nothing more than "figments of a felonious imagination." So you see, one way to get anything you want out of life, even in New York City, is to ask enough people to hand over their money to you.

What was the offer that induced people to trust this one-time bank employee and former securities manager? They were told that if they invested their money with him, they could earn 18 to 20 percent a year in interest, risk free!

Because that was more than three times the prevailing rate for a no-risk return, it's not surprising that people who wanted to get rich quickly invested more than $4 million in a plan with nonexistent investments and profits. But when even a few investors wanted their original investment and earned interest payments returned to them in cash, the house of cards collapsed and the investors lost all their "risk-free" money. The money they had invested had already been spent on a lifestyle that even a sultan could envy. But though the Securities and Exchange Commission (SEC) might catch the wrongdoers, it is not empowered to recover and return any fraud losses to investors.

These financial scams are named after a Boston swindler named Charles (Carlo) Ponzi. He came as an immigrant to New York City in 1903 at the age of 20, penniless and unable to speak English. By 1920, he had moved to Boston, where he established a worthless company with the imposing name of "Securities Exchange Company."

At a time when Boston banks were paying 4 percent annual interest, Ponzi claimed that he could buy postal coupons overseas and sell them in America at huge profits and he offered "investments" redeemable in 90 days at 50 percent interest. The newspapers were quick to point out that there weren't enough postal coupons in the world to make that kind of money, but eager investors nevertheless poured as much as $15 million into the Securities Exchange Company.

But the scheme could continue to work, Ponzi knew, only as long as the interest earned by previous investors was paid out of the money received from subsequent investors. When that was not possible, the so-called investors lost everything. What greedy investors have learned, when they take the bait on a deal that is too good to be true, is that it's not enough to be the first one in on a Ponzi scheme; you have to be the first one out as well.

After you've been on the air and in the financial world for more than 30 years, you'd think that nothing would surprise you, that you have heard it all. But even I was surprised when I was on the radio in New York, and one of the hottest investment scams of the year was selling dirt that, if refined, would contain gold. You could, the story went, invest and receive gold for a mere $250 an ounce. The lure of gold was too much for many people to resist, and after the scam artists had collected millions of dollars from would-be goldbugs, it turned out that the promoters were selling plain dirt that contained no more gold than seawater. And, as if that weren't enough, it would cost more to transport the dirt to the mill than anyone could expect to find in gold.

Security regulators say another big problem with some stock promoters is the "pump and dump" scam. These people use newsletters and radio and newspaper ads to sell stock at inflated prices. The scam operators grabbed the stock for almost nothing and the increased sales to new investors tends to push up the price of the stock. When the scam collapses, the investors are left holding worthless shares of stock.

What also surprises me, as more and more people are taken by scams, is that people never learn. Each year billions of dollars are lost by investors who forget that if something sounds too good to be true, it probably is.

If you're about to join the "in crowd" who knows someone who can triple the return you can get anywhere else, or who has a hot stock or a pile of dirt just waiting to make you rich, what you're going to read next is embarrassingly simple:

- First, check out the offer with a financial planner or accountant before you trust your money to someone you don't know. Otherwise, you could be left to shoulder the loss—money you may be depending on to fund your retirement.

- Be aware that by using false authorization letters, scam artists can transfer your investments to bank accounts under their own name. Once you receive reports, be sure to check out where the statements came from and follow up immediately to verify the performance returns. Also, be sure your assets are available should you want the money returned.

Be aware that your glowing returns could be based on falsified brokerage or other in-house statements. Worse yet, these falsified statements could entitle the scam artist to collect hefty fees and commissions even though the scam had incurred substantial losses.

Remember, if the offer sounds too good to be true, if it will make you more money than anything you've found in your search to build wealth, you're better off *making and keeping* money the old-fashioned way. After all, it's not how much you'll make on your money, but whether your money will ever be returned to you.

LESSON 8
The Power of Determination
Compounding

*"For most people, more than 90 percent of their
retirement nest egg will be made on money
they never invested or saved."*

A 73-year-old man made the 240-mile trip to visit his 80-year-old brother, who was ill, driving his lawn mower all the way. He chose to use his John Deere riding mower as his vehicle because he didn't have a driver's license. Hitched to the back of the mower was a trailer in which he hauled supplies and camping equipment. He averaged only five miles an hour, and the trip took six weeks.

What I discovered a long time ago, along with the man on the lawn mower, is that if you really want to do something, chances are you can. If you want to become wealthy, and you stick with your plan, you can. The problem is that most people underestimate what they can do with a plan and a few bucks a day. They think becoming rich at retirement is beyond their reach.

"But Jim," I have been told, "I only have a few hundred dollars to invest and it won't make any difference anyway."

Don't laugh. You've probably said this before. Almost everyone has. But it's not true. There are a lot of distractions as we plow through life, but I'm reminded of a story I was once told by a man who saved a few dollars each day. He was a penny-pincher who believed that a penny saved was a penny earned. He never missed the few bucks he saved, he invested each day, and today he's retired with a hefty income. I'll never forget what he told me about the secret of how he saved his money: "I don't buy things because I have money; I buy things because I need them."

How did he build his wealth? Beginning at age 35, he invested just $200 a month in good growth stock mutual funds and continued to do this until he reached age 65. Over this 30-year period, he had invested a total of only $72,000, yet his retirement nest egg had grown to more than $1 million. The important lesson to learn here is that *more than 90 percent of his retirement nest egg was made on money he'd never saved or invested in the first place.*

A man in Chicago called in to my radio show and said, "You know, this really works! It's crazy, but I'm now making more on my nest-egg buildup each year than I make in my salary."

Try to visualize it this way: To make a loaf of bread you let the dough rise. The bread gets bigger over time. You don't do anything; the yeast makes it rise. That's the same way your money grows in a stock mutual fund. Instead of yeast, it's the incredible power of compounding over time— often called the 8th wonder of the world—the reinvestment of dividends, or the money earned each year, and the rise in the value of the stock market. With savings of even $200 a month, this accumulation of wealth can go a long way toward paying your living expenses once you retire. Remember, just a few bucks a day from the cookie jar where you put your spare cash will do the job.

LESSON 9
The Ant and the Elephant
IRA Plans

Millionaire publisher Steve Forbes spent millions of his own money to run for the Republican nomination for president in 1996. He said from the start that he didn't expect to win the nomination, but he wanted to tell people about the flat tax and how it could move millions of workers off the tax rolls, enable millions more to file their tax returns on a postcard, jump-start the economy, and create jobs.

This story reminds me of the old Yogi Berra adage, that "it's *deja vu* all over again." And it is. In 1913, when income taxes were first levied in this country, Form 1040 was four pages long and the IRS code was 400 pages. There was a flat tax, 95 percent of workers were exempt from paying taxes, and most of the rest paid a flat 1 percent on their income. Today, the IRS code is 80,000 pages long and you often need a crystal ball and a professional adviser in order to figure out what you owe.

Over the years, Congress has engaged in what is commonly called "social and economic engineering." The government has placed higher marginal tax rates on those with high incomes and added new wrinkles for tax deductions that would force individuals and corporations to spend, save, and invest in the ways the government wanted. In addition, to appease the voters back home, Congress also frequently simplifies the tax code. Take the historic tax reform act signed more than a decade ago by President Reagan. The law was a politician's dream. It reduced the number of tax rates, cut the top personal income tax rate, and wiped out most tax shelters. But now, a decade later, the tax code is almost right back where it started, with mind-numbing complexity from the number of changes. The top marginal tax rate paid at the time of passage of that tax reform was 28 percent, but it has risen again to about 40 percent today.

With all this game-playing and constant changing of the tax rules, Americans have the world's most complicated income tax system. At the same time, we have tax loopholes that let knowledgeable people legally escape or delay most or all of their taxes, while others fall victim to the often bewildering tax rules. Here are some examples.

During my seminars, I paint a word picture of a guy entering a second marriage and waiting for his bride at the altar. As she moves down the aisle, he suddenly remembers that he previously sold his home and used the $125,000 tax exclusion, but she has a home and she has not used the exclusion. His heart sinks with every step she takes because, once they are married, she becomes what the IRS calls a "tainted spouse." If she sells her house *before* marriage to him, she can use the $125,000 tax exclusion (over age 55, lived in the home for three of the past five years), but once they are married, she loses this hefty tax advantage because she is now married to someone who has previously used the exclusion.

Or consider this. Because the bridegroom is not covered by a retirement plan at work, he wants to make a tax-deductible Individual Retirement Account contribution this year. But as his bride approaches the altar, he visualizes his tax deduction going up in smoke. She has a job and is covered in a company retirement plan, and if they are married for *only one day* during the year, they are *both* considered covered under her retirement plan and he's no longer eligible to deduct IRA contributions because together they will earn more than the allowable limit. Our bridegroom also remembers the wedding is in December. They both work and will now pay the "marriage tax" this year (singles pay less in taxes than marrieds).

The point of this lesson is that getting married for lust or money can be a good idea, but for most people, it helps to wander through the tax code before tying the knot.

With all these silly tax rules, you may feel like an ant being crushed by the IRS elephant, and if you do, you're not alone. The tax code is so complicated that *Money* magazine's annual contest, which asks 50 professional tax preparers how much a hypothetical family would owe in taxes, ends up with a wide range of different tax bills. In my own case, I never know how much I owe in taxes until I get the tax returns back from my accountant and I have to trust him to figure it all out.

One thing most of us agree on is that since 1913, Congress has greatly hiked federal income taxes for nearly everybody. The result, says the Tax Foundation, is that the average American pays more annually in taxes than for food, clothing, and shelter *combined*. Over the years, I've seen both my income and my tax rate rise, but never before has it been more important to avoid and delay taxes. If you don't factor in taxes as you build your wealth and your retirement nest egg, your savings can resemble the size of an ant. And, if you aren't careful, the IRS can even step on the ant. If, on the other hand, you play within the rules and legally avoid or delay taxes, your nest egg can resemble the size of an elephant.

But playing by the changing rules can be difficult. Over the years, Congress has authorized a tidal wave of different retirement plans and the rules have changed whenever Congress needed more money. For example, when Individual Retirement Accounts first appeared in 1974 for people not covered by a retirement plan at work, not many people were interested. To encourage more people to open IRAs, Congress made the deal even sweeter with the passage of the Economic Recovery Tax Act of 1981, which allowed *all* working Americans to make tax-deductible contributions.

Then, to raise more tax revenue, Congress changed the 1981 IRA rules in the 1986 Tax Reform Act, so that many working people who were covered by a retirement plan at work were once again denied a tax-deductible way to save on their own. Then in 1996, before the elections, Congress boosted the annual tax-deductible contribution for a nonworking spouse to $2,000, from the old limit of $250. But the new rules still require you to qualify for deductible contributions, and that depends on your income level and whether or not you are covered by a retirement plan at work.

Because the tax-deduction rules for IRAs have become so complicated, many people think they don't qualify for a tax-deductible IRA. But your success in building a retirement nest egg begins with your understanding of the rules. Once you do, any contribution to an IRA is a "no-brainer" decision.

Here's how the IRA rules work:

- Your contributions can come only from "earned income" through wages, salary, self-employment income, professional fees, bonuses, tips, and alimony. Income that doesn't count includes such items as interest and dividends, pension and retirement plan income, rental income, and capital gains on the sale of securities or property.

- The maximum annual contribution to a regular IRA is $2,000, or up to 100 percent of your earned income not to exceed $2,000. Nonworking spouses can also contribute up to a maximum of $2,000. However, you can't make contributions to an IRA with earned income if you are over the age of 70½.

Now comes the hard part: determining if you can take a tax deduction.

- If you and/or your spouse are not an "active participant" in an employer-sponsored retirement plan at work (not even for one day during the year), you can take the maximum allowable deduction regardless of your income.

- If you and/or your spouse are an active participant in an employer-sponsored retirement plan and your adjusted gross income (AGI) on your Form 1040 is less than $40,000 for married couples filing jointly, or $25,000 for an individual, you can also take the maximum allowable deduction.

But if you are covered under a company-sponsored retirement plan and your AGI is more than $50,000 for a married couple filing jointly, or $35,000 for an individual, then you can't take any IRA deduction at all.

"What a mess!" Bob complained to me one day toward the end of the year. "Look, I'm covered by some kind of retirement plan at work," he said, "and I don't have any idea if I can get a tax deduction for my IRA this year. Heck, I don't even know if it's worth the hassle."

"Bob, there's a price for doing nothing, and you can pay the price now or you can pay it later. How much will you and your wife make this year?" I asked.

"Somewhere around $45,000. Why do you ask?"

"Because with that income you are a 'transition' worker and you can still get a tax deduction for an IRA. Married, your transition is between $40,000 and $50,000 of income."

"You got to be kidding me," Bob seared. "Who thought this crazy game up?"

"Congress."

"I might have guessed," he said.

"But don't give up. Even if your annual income exceeds the limits for a maximum deduction, you may still be eligible for a partial IRA deduction. The handy rule is that for each additional $50 of income earned between $25,000 and $35,000 for an individual, and between $40,000 and

$50,000 for a married couple, your annual deductible amount is reduced by $10."

Here's how Bob can figure his allowable tax-deductible IRA contribution when he is married with an AGI of $45,000:

Enter his total income	$45,000
Deduct his total income from the maximum limit of $50,000	$ 5,000
Multiply by 20 percent (.20 × $5,000)	$ 1,000

In this case, he and his working wife can divide up a $1,000 deductible contribution as they wish. Because his allowable contribution is one half the regular contribution of $2,000, if Bob had a nonworking spouse, she could take half the regular $2,000 spousal IRA deduction, or a $1,000 tax deduction. In the weird world of IRA rules, when Bob and his wife both work, their combined annual tax-deductible contribution under this example is limited to $1,000, but if only one spouse works outside the home the couple's annual limit is $2,000.

Another important factor I've learned in making IRA contributions is to make them as soon as you can each year. While most people put off their contributions to year-end or when they file their tax returns, the sooner your money starts earning and benefiting from compounding in a tax-free environment, the larger your retirement nest egg. Not by just a bit, but by a big chunk over the years.

LESSON 10
Don't Kill the Goose
Investing in Retirement Plans

The chances are that your employer has offered you the opportunity to participate in a company-sponsored retirement plan. There is also a good possibility that you've been offered a matching plan where you can grab free company money. Here's my advice to you: When the IRS and your employer give you a goose that lays golden eggs, keep it on the nest laying eggs as long as you can. But the terrible truth is that rather than saving money for their employer's matching plan, many people kill the golden goose before it has a chance to help them build their nest egg. So, if you want to build wealth today, your job is to sock away as much as you can from your paycheck into your company's retirement plan, grab the free matching money, and avoid killing the company goose before it has finished laying its golden eggs.

While I'm at it, I should tell you another lesson I've learned about building wealth. It came from a man I met several years ago who asked me to review his portfolio. As I looked at the amount of money he had in his IRA and 401(k) plan, I felt like roadkill on the highway to prosperity. He had almost $1 million in his retirement plans. He told me that if I saved money, used tax-deferred retirement plans, and took advantage of my employer's matching contributions, I too could become rich. I took his advice, I never killed the golden goose, and I've never regretted it.

Here's how he described building wealth: "Think of a 401(k) plan at work as a cardboard box in your living room with the words 'tax-deferred' printed on each side. Every dollar of your paycheck you toss into the box escapes current income taxes. If, on the other hand, you pay your taxes and pocket what's left of your wages in your wallet or purse, you'll have a great deal less than you earned."

From a practical point of view, let me tell you what can happen when you contribute $3,000 a year ($250 a month) from your paycheck into your 401(k) plan with a 50¢ on-the-dollar match from your employer. Assume that your investments in stock mutual funds grow only 10 percent a year, and you're in a 30 percent combined federal and state tax bracket. By investing in a 401(k) plan and delaying taxes, your balance at the end of the first year could be $4,950. On your own, paying taxes, your balance is only $2,247.

This is not a figment of the imagination. At the end of the first year, inside that cardboard box, you actually invested $3,000 and ended up with almost $5,000. I'm certain that the bib overall farmers I knew in my youth would jump at the chance of turning $3,000 into $5,000 in one year. From a practical point of view, if you continue to contribute the same $3,000 each year with your employer's match, in five years your 401(k) plan should total about $30,000, while on your own, after paying taxes, you would have only about $13,000.

What I'm about to tell you next is the secret of building real wealth on a budget. And this lesson is one I've told a thousand times because it's worked for me and it can work for you. If you continued to put $3,000 a year into your 401(k) plan for five years with the same employer match, you could have earned, on average, $6,000 a year toward your retirement nest egg!

I know you are thinking it's too good to be true. Besides, taxes have to be paid on the 401(k) money before it can be used in retirement. But using this example, if you have at least ten years to retirement, tax-sheltering your income and growth in stock mutual funds over the long haul should give you more after-tax money than paying taxes each year and investing the difference. The reason? The power of tax-deferred compounding over time and the possible boost you'll get from the employer's extra pay-ins. In a nutshell, you can almost always accumulate more spending money on a tax-deferred basis and, even after paying taxes down the road, you'll have more money to spend in retirement.

But what if your employer offers company stock with a hefty matching program? My advice is don't go overboard in stuffing your 401(k) plan with your company's stock. Today, according to the Institute of Management and Administration, a startling 42 percent of the money Americans have funneled into 401(k) plans and similar retirement programs has been invested in company stock. When the SEC has limited "diversified" mutual funds to investing no more than five percent of their assets in one company, investors are taking a lot more risk than they realize by investing most of their assets in their company stock.

If you already have a 401(k) or other company retirement plan stuffed with your company's stock, here are some reasons that illustrate why it's important to understand the mysterious and mind-boggling rules of the IRS before you make a job move. If you cash out the stock and take the money, the IRS can cut your assets like a high-powered weed-whacker. You'll pay income taxes on the current market value of the stock, not the original price you paid when you purchased the stock. If you roll over the company stock into an IRA to continue to defer taxes—and, in some cases, to avoid the 10 percent early withdrawal penalty—that too could be a mistake.

I should make it clear right now that I don't make up the IRS tax rules. They were made up by people in Washington who I suspect never realized how complicated and unfair these rules could become.

If you don't sell the stock and keep it outside an IRA when you change jobs, you'll owe income taxes only on their "cost basis," which is on the value of the shares at the time they were added to your retirement plan account. Holding the stock yourself, you will, of course, pay income taxes on the dividends, but the unrealized appreciation (capital gains) won't be taxable until you sell the stock. Keeping the stock outside an IRA also lets you play the tax game in other ways:

- When you die, your heirs will owe no income taxes on any gains in the company stock, except the gains before you took out the shares from the retirement plan. That's because assets, except IRAs and annuities, get a "stepped-up" basis to current market value at death. If the stock was inherited from an IRA, the total amount received would be taxable to the heirs.
- You can avoid mandatory distributions at age 70½, which an IRA requires.
- If later on the stock price plunges and you sell, you can deduct your losses, which you can't do in an IRA.

The retirement plan you can join will depend on where you work and how you earn your paycheck, but you have a wide choice of tax-deferred retirement plans: an IRA; for the self-employed (and their employees), a Simplified Employee Pension (SEP-IRA) plan, a Keogh plan, and a Defined Benefit Keogh plan; for employees, a Savings Incentive Match Plan for Employees (SIMPLE), a 401(k), a pension, a profit-sharing plan, and an Employee Stock Ownership Plan (ESOP); for nonprofit employees and school teachers, a 403(b) plan; and for public employees, a 457 plan.

With all these opportunities to save for retirement, what has bothered me for years is that this array of retirement plans makes a mockery of any attempt at fairness to all American workers. Under our complex tax laws, the size of the annual deductible retirement plan contribution is based not on fairness, but on *where* the individual works and how much he or she knows about the various options that are available.

To get an idea of how disparate retirement plans can be, consider this scenario: Four workers enter an elevator. One says, "I have a 403(b) retirement plan at work and I take a tax deduction right off the top of my salary for almost 20 percent of my pay. I can boost my deductions because I'm making up for past years when I couldn't make contributions when we were raising the children."

"Not bad," says another worker. "I have a 401(k) where my employer matches my contributions dollar for dollar. With my company's help, I sock away about $12,000 a year, of which only half is my own money." "I can top that," says another. "I'm self-employed and I have a defined benefit retirement plan, so I take a tax deduction for more than half my income."

The fourth worker looks at the floor as the elevator continues to rise. "My company has a profit-sharing plan," he says, "and with business so poor, I'll be lucky if the company puts $500 into my plan by year-end. On top of that, I can't even make a tax-deductible contribution to my IRA."

I should tell you about another rule. It's not my rule, it came from my father. He was not a Scrooge, but I knew he counted every penny he had. He told me, "There will come a time when you are faced with the question of whether you should spend your money or save it. Spend it," he said, "if you need the money to live on, but save it if you want to build wealth." That deceptively simple choice is one we all face, but to live well in retirement, you need to use the help of your employer and put your money to work using "the magic of compounding" by earning money on the money you've already invested.

Everybody has a dream about retirement and your dream can start by socking away a few dollars from your paycheck into your employer's retirement plan. I can promise you that after a few years, you'll feel a lot better about yourself and that something really good can happen after all. Just think what you could do if *you* saved $3,000 a year in a 401(k) "cardboard box" and you had 20 years until retirement.

LESSON 11
If I Had My Life to Live Over
The Importance of Dividends

*"In a nutshell, reinvesting your dividends
in a stock fund is the glue that holds
your financial plan together."*

If I had my life to live over, I'd think more about putting all the pieces together before I tried to build success. As a kid, when I played mud pies with my sister in our backyard, she knew more about success than I did. While I was busy grabbing the mud to build ever-larger mud pies, she hogged the water. Ever try to make a mud pie without water?

This brings me to another common mistake many investors make: trying to build a retirement nest egg without dividends. Believe me, it's like trying to build mud pies without water. The concept I want to share with you in this lesson is the importance of reinvesting your dividends. In a nutshell, reinvesting your dividends in a stock mutual fund is the glue that holds your financial plan together.

"What's the most important thing you can do after you've invested in mutual funds?" a caller boomed out over the airwaves on my radio show. Without hesitation, I answered: "Keep all your money working all the time."

I have given this answer to many listeners over the years, but I doubt if they really know the importance of keeping all their money at work. Keeping your hands off your stock fund dividends may not seem like a big deal, until you realize that over a 15-year period, the difference between taking out your dividends and reinvesting them is enormous.

Here's how it works: From 1979 to 1994, a one-time hypothetical $10,000 investment in the Standard & Poor's 500 stock index would have grown to about $44,000. But over this same period, if you reinvested all your dividends as they were paid, the total return would have soared to about $75,000. That sounds absurd, doesn't it? I have almost twice the retirement nest egg than I would have had simply because I left the dividends alone.

Most people think of making money in the stock market when the Dow Jones Industrial Average rises. But this lesson may come across better when you consider that dividends can be as important as what you make on your investment from rising stock prices. For example, from July 1, 1946 to June 30, 1996 more than 87 percent of an investor's total return in the Standard & Poor's 500 stock index came from reinvested dividend income.

Dividends are truly the jumper cables of the investment world. Even if you're otherwise financially illiterate, if you save in a disciplined way and invest often, reinvesting dividends each time they are paid can jump-start your investment portfolio like nothing else. Obviously, it follows that *if you need to withdraw money from time to time, don't invest in a stock mutual fund.*

Millions of people don't understand this simple concept of making money by reinvesting dividends. And just think, you didn't have to read a ton of books or learn any hot new money-managing ideas to grasp this important concept of building wealth. I don't worry about the big picture, I can handle that stuff without breaking stride. What concerns me is the small stuff, and doing that right is what counts.

LESSON 12
Shopping at Wal-Mart
Saving for a Rainy Day

Today, millions of people earning good incomes spend their money like there is no tomorrow. But tomorrow can come in the form of a crushing downsizing and the loss of a job. It makes no difference which spouse suddenly becomes unemployed, the results can often be the same.

"Well, if it isn't Jack Robertson," I said as the jogging figure came alongside of me. Dressed in a fancy jogging suit with the maker's name flashing across his chest and his feet bouncing along in air-pumped-up running shoes, he slowed down to match my more modest speed.

"I'm glad I caught you this morning," he said. "I need your help. I made a good salary but I could never get out of debt and I didn't save anything for the future."

"Maybe you should have been shopping at Wal-Mart," I said, glancing at his $100 running clothes, "and pay off your debts. Then maybe you could save some money for the future. The money you are spending that you don't have is killing you."

"I know," he said, "but my paycheck runs out next week. I've lost my job."

The next time I saw Jack, he told me he was trying to avoid bankruptcy, but he was losing the battle. In less than four months after losing his job, Jack was frantically chasing white-collar jobs in a market that downsizing had already filled with unemployed executives, and he had used his credit cards to the tune of $15,000. He had given up his fancy car because he couldn't afford the payments, and he no longer spent more than $500 a month in fancy restaurants.

"You know," he said, "we were doing just fine on a big fat salary, but after I lost my job we were wiped out almost instantly. Now, we'll probably lose our home."

"That could be a problem," I said. "How much do you owe on your mortgage and what is your home worth?"

"Well, we bought the home for $275,000 and then we got a home-equity loan to pay off some debts, and with that loan and our mortgage, our debt is about $250,000. I think we can sell the home for maybe $225,000 if we are lucky."

"I hope you're lucky," I said, "because if you walk away from your debts the IRS says getting excused from paying a debt is the economic equivalent of receiving the same amount in cash, and the IRS requires anyone so excused to treat that amount as taxable income."

"You mean I'll have to pay income taxes on the difference?"

"That's right. If you get lucky and sell the home for $225,000 with a mortgage and a loan of $250,000, you'd owe income taxes on $25,000 of so-called income."

Jack shook his head. "But don't they realize that I don't have the money?"

"Good question, but I don't think the IRS cares. And I have some more bad news. You can't deduct that $50,000 loss on the purchase and sale of your home because the IRS doesn't consider your home an investment."

Jack still wears his fancy jogging clothes, but—and I swear this is true—he does shop at Wal-Mart now and he now spends less than he earns. Here is the moral of this lesson: If you don't save for a rainy day, the best umbrella won't protect you from your creditors.

LESSON 13

Lessons from a Farmer on How to Save

One day after I finished my high school classes, I walked over to the farm equipment store where my dad was keeping track of the books. The temperature had risen to over 100°F. I could tell it was going to be another sizzler because the black repair tar in the center of the street had already begun to melt. I reached into the five-cent Coke machine, dipped my hand into the ice water, and took out a bottle.

The farmers were talking about the new tractors, the hayrakes, and money. I drew closer to listen to their words, not because I was interested in anything about hayrakes, but because I knew these farmers in our town always had money. And money in my youth was a precious commodity.

It was easy to tell the farmers from the salesmen: the farmers wore bib overalls. Not just any overalls, mind you. The garment of choice, as far as I could tell, had the logo "Oshkosh B Gosh" sewn on the top flap.

Farmers are a strange bunch. You pretend to be comfortable with them, but you never are. They know it, but they also pretend they don't. But much of what I learned about how to accumulate wealth and build a cash reserve came from talking with these farmers.

If I had to wrap up all the financial planning ideas in the world, they could be boiled down to one simple premise told to me over a hayrake in an equipment store: First, save some money the safe way, and then take some risks for the years ahead. That's the whole deal and it worked for the farmers. Everyone in our small town knew they were rich: They paid cash and they drove big Cadillacs.

So I asked one of these farmers, "How did you save money and get so rich?"

"Well, sonny," he said, looking me straight in the eyes, "if you don't pay yourself first, no one else will."

"Is that all there is to getting rich?" I asked.

"That's it," he said. "Lord knows you don't have to be smart. You don't have to make a lot of money. But if you don't save *some* money each month, all the fancy investment advice in the world won't make you rich. Remember," he said, "nobody has ever gone broke with money in the bank."

I was on a roll now so I went for the good stuff. "If I'm not being too personal," I said, "how did you learn to pay yourself first?"

"The problem most people face is that they can't save any money because no one has sent them a bill. To get started, I made up a bunch of bills, put them in envelopes addressed to me, and gave them to a friend. Each month he dropped one in the mail and I paid the bill to the bank. I learned never to miss the money. I got really good at this," he said with a smile, "and now I can pay cash for anything I want."

Dreaming of a time when I might get rich, I asked the farmer: "How will I know when I'm rich like you?"

As a high school student ready to make my way to college and my fortune, I'll never forget his answer: "You know you are rich," he said, "when you can afford anything you want and you don't want anything."

By now my mind was working overtime as I listened to the farmer and I began to envision a time when, like him, I too could pay cash and drive a Cadillac. After all, if you didn't need to be smart, and if you didn't have to make a lot of money, I knew I had a head start on most people.

LESSON 14

The Magic of Guessing
Timing the Market

Before we moved to California, where I attended high school, I spent my grade school years in Omaha, Nebraska. Each year my parents told me my summer vacation was to live on a relative's farm in Iowa. My mother said she knew

I'd have fun on the farm, but I think her real reason was she needed a vacation from me. At the time of my visit, the farmhouse still had the party-line telephone in the kitchen, the cream separator on the back porch, and dinner might include a chicken that lost its head with one swing of an ax. In my second-floor bedroom, I started a journal so I could tell my friends in school what it was like to live on a farm. Now, years later, as I look through the frayed pages of this journal, I see a note in bold letters: "I always get stuck with the nasty jobs!" Without a car, without a driver's license, and without money to spend, I could be depended on to clean the cream separator and the chicken coop.

What made cleaning out the chicken coop so nasty was that we put ground-up corncobs on the floor and when they were soaked with manure they weighed a ton. It was backbreaking work and each night, after a turn in the chicken coop, every fiber in my body ached. Today you have to tell your kids you love them just to get them to take out the garbage.

I also sat in the barn and watched the animals. For a grade school kid from the big city, this was great stuff. The Holsteins and Guernseys, which I helped milk, had two jobs: to give milk and give birth. When this cycle played out, the cow was dead meat. But no one knew exactly when the next birth would occur.

When I got to Wall Street, I realized that the brokers and the stock mutual fund managers, who virtually read their tea leaves to forecast the market and divine the time when stocks were going to rise and fall, did about as well as someone sitting in a barn trying to time the birth of a calf.

But millions of people continue to think they can do better investing with the advice of people who sit in offices guessing when the next hot stock will appear or a market decline will occur. Or, they believe they can make big bucks with the help of expensive financial newsletters, or buying some mutual fund that just set a new performance record in South America. I admit, I sometimes get little flashes of fantasies about striking it big with a new fund or stock. But, unless the lightning bolt of dumb luck strikes me, I'll probably end up losing my stake and thinking up some clever explanation of why I eat at McDonald's.

The Super Bowl comes only once a year, but for the more than 300 investment newsletter writers, it comes with every issue. For around $250 a year, their job is to tell you when to buy or sell your stocks or mutual funds. These market-timers frantically try to outsmart the market and make money for their subscribers. But I'll let you in on another secret: Investment newsletters rarely beat the guy who buys and holds good stock mutual funds and never reads any financial letters. Year after year, only a tiny handful of these newsletter writers beat the average returns of the stock market.

When investment newsletter writers try to time the market, they do a terrible job of telling you when they guessed wrong and when their advice cost you a bundle. But they don't have to; several newsletters make it their business to report the actual results of following other newsletters' advice. How good are investment newsletters at picking stocks and mutual funds? Not very good, according to Mark Hulbert, who writes the *Hulbert Financial Digest,* a newsletter that tracks the performance of investment newsletters.

According to his newsletter, which uses the Wilshire 5000, an index of all stocks traded on the three major exchanges as a benchmark, over the 15 previous years ending December 18, 1996, only four of the mutual fund newsletters he tracks beat the total return of the Wilshire 5000 stock index. Over the past five and eight years, five newsletters did.

Or, consider the *Timer Digest's* Top Ten Timers for one year from October 1995 to October 1996. The performance is calculated by considering each newsletter and the Standard & Poor's 500 stock index to be equal at the beginning of the period. During this one-year period, only three investment newsletters tracked by the *Digest* beat the S&P 500 stock index. For the previous six months, the newsletters did even worse: Only two newsletters beat the S&P 500 stock index.

Almost all mutual fund portfolio managers don't do any better; they also fail to match the overall average of the entire stock market. The newest idea to beat the market average is to offer a mutual fund managed by so-called "world-class" money managers in which each manager would be limited to between five and ten of their favorite stocks. Then, it is reasoned, investors could get good overall diversification from the best fund managers who would specialize in their own special field of stock-picking.

This set me to thinking about how fund managers work. Most of them would do better for their shareholders if they just invested in some good blue chip stocks, or some stock market index, turned out the lights, and went home.

For example, it turns out that the portfolio managers of Fidelity Investments, the nation's largest family of mutual funds, left the lights on. *Time* magazine's cover story (September 30, 1996) asks, "Can Fidelity Still Make Your Money Grow?" All 12 of its largest funds were trailing the stock market, lagging behind the benchmark S&P 500 stock index for the current year. *Time* asks, "If you can't beat an average with any more skill than you would if you chose stocks randomly, how hard is it to beat the S&P 500? Really hard," says *Time.*

You know what I'm going to tell you. I know you do. I'm going to tell you that with all those analysts, stock-pickers, market forecasters, and Wall Street gurus, Fidelity's flagship fund, the Magellan Fund, according to Lipper Analytical Services, had a total return with dividends reinvested in 1996 of 11.7 percent. The general stock fund's average return for 1996 did better, up 19.1 percent. On the other hand, simply investing in the Standard & Poor's 500 stock index fund and earning average market returns, with dividends reinvested, the gain for 1996 was 22.7 percent.

Investing in the S&P 500 stock index fund and sitting on your hands may appear to be old-fashioned to many investors, but it works. According to Morningstar, the Chicago tracking firm that rates mutual funds, only four of the nation's 25 largest funds, which have close to $500 billion in assets, outperformed the Standard & Poor's 500 stock index average return. Over the past 15 years, only 11 of the popular growth and income stock funds have beaten the S&P 500 stock index.

One of the best books on investing is *A Random Walk Down Wall Street,* by Burton G. Malkiel (1996, sixth edition; published by W.W. Norton & Company). Malkiel is a professor at Princeton University and serves as a governor on the American Stock Exchange. Watching the market day after day, it dawned on him that investing is really a simple process. A random walk, he said, is one in which you can't predict future actions on past results. Malkiel believes that all the chart readers and investment gurus who try to guess the future of the stock market based on past experiences are wasting their time.

His book offers the following conclusion: "On Wall Street, the term 'random walk' is an obscenity. It is an epithet coined by the academic world and hurled insultingly at the professional soothsayers. Taken to its logical extreme, it means that a blindfolded monkey throwing darts at a newspaper's financial pages could select a portfolio that would do just as well as one carefully selected by the experts."

I think of Malkiel every time I read the *Wall Street Journal's* regular six-month investment dartboard contest in which the paper pits the performance of four investment professionals against stocks chosen by *Wall Street Journal* staffers tossing darts at the *Journal's* stock tables. As if they have leaped from the pages of Malkiel's book, the forces of chance regularly wallop the pros.

If you think this sounds absurd, let me tell you about one of the best market-timers over the past few years, Arch Crawford. He writes the *Crawford Perspectives* and, according to the *Timer Digest,* he was the "timer of the year" for 1992, the number one timer for 1994, and number two for the first six months of 1995. He was also the four-year top timer in the bond market. Mark Hulbert, editor of the *Hulbert Financial Digest,* a monthly service that monitors the performance of investment advisory newsletters, says Arch Crawford is the number one market-timer over a five-year period. In his story in *Forbes* magazine (September 11, 1995), Hulbert writes: "I'm not festooning my office wall with astrological charts or staying up late nights with the work of Nostradamus. I am only saying that results are what count and, since results are what Arch Crawford has produced, I will take him seriously—whatever I may think about astrology."

And astrology is the way Arch Crawford gets the results that hundreds of other market-timing newsletter writers and mutual fund portfolio managers would die for. He does his market timing by planetary cycles and astrology. One day in 1992, Arch published a buy signal three days before the stock market took off like a rocket. And then he later gave a sell signal just before one of the largest declines in history. Each time, multiple planetary alignments took place.

When Jupiter aligns with Mars, or when the next eclipse occurs, Arch Crawford can tell you what it means for your investments and beat the performance of all but a few lucky market-timers who base their forecasts on the economy, interest rates, and corporate profits.

"I don't know about you," a market watcher told me, "but if sunspots or piles of junk in my garage can foretell the future, I have to take notice. Right now watching the heavens seems to be hot."

████████

LESSON 15
Meet the Gang
How Much People Make in the Stock Market

I belong to a group of men who meet once a week for breakfast at Millie's. The restaurant is in an old house and the wooden tables and chairs look like they came from a Goodwill store. Maybe it's the cozy surroundings, or maybe it's the same food we order each week (my favorite is French toast), but whatever it is we trade stories, catch up on the news, and drink coffee.

Not long ago the subject of making money in the stock market came up. I was ready for this, of course, and I asked, "How much do you think people who have been investing in the stock market for the past five years have been making on average each year?" Thinking of a savings account, Bill answered, "Maybe 5 or 6 percent a year." "The answer," I said with a knowing grin, "is about 15 percent."

Bill looked at me with disgust. "What is that, some new way of making money?"

By the confused looks on their faces, I could tell that an example was in order. "It's not new," I said. "Here's how it works. The first lesson to learn is that the stock market jumps up and down each year, and unlike an insured certificate of deposit you're not sure just what you'll earn each year."

"So," Bill told the group with a knowing grin, "I don't really know if I'll make any money each year. Is that what you are saying?"

"That's exactly what I'm saying," I replied, "but you don't have to take a Maalox before you go to bed every night. History tells us that you will do very well *over the years*. Let's start with the last few years. Say you invested $10,000 and just got the stock market averages, as measured by the Standard & Poor's 500 stock index. In 1993, the total return was 10 percent. The next year, 1994, the market went into the tank over higher interest rates and you made a little over 1 percent, even less than passbook savings rates. Then in 1995, the S&P 500 index was up almost 38 percent. In 1996, the index was up 23 percent. Even if the S&P 500 stock index returns only 5 percent in 1997, the five-year average annual total return would be more than 15 percent. Over those five years, if you left your investment alone and reinvested the dividends, your original investment of $10,000 could have turned into more than $20,000."

"That's really a sweet deal," John broke in, "but it still sounds like some story on Microsoft and Bill Gates. Are you sure you have your figures straight?"

"Yes," I replied. "Over the past 15 or so years, the S&P 500 stock index has *averaged* about a 15 percent total return each year, so this five-year period is no exception. But what most people don't realize is just how much money they make over time in the stock market with compounding."

"I'm interested," John said, "tell me more."

"Well, the punch line is coming and it's a beaut. Without any new investments in the stock mutual fund, based on recent history, your entire nest egg has a chance to double about every five years. But, in order for your nest egg to double in five years, your average annual compounded return has to be 20 percent!

"Look at it this way," I said, "the average annual compounded gain of 20 percent sure beats the 5 percent you can make on an insured certificate of deposit."

Finally, lightning struck in the eyes of the guys around the table. John looked at me in awe. "You mean to tell me," he said, "that some people in the stock market have made as much in one year as I've made in four years at the bank?"

"I'm afraid so," I said.

"All right, let's cut out the small talk. Tell me how much I need to save and invest each year to have $100,000 at age 65."

"You have 15 years to age 65," I told John, "and if the market continues to average a 15 percent total return each year (and no one knows if it will), you'd need to invest $2,102 each year. Makes an IRA look kinda good, doesn't it?"

One of my companions, with pancakes on his fork, took a gulp of his coffee and said, "Well, fellows, the fixed-savings dogs don't bark, do they?"

Once again, you've learned one of the magic lessons of Wall Street: money and time can make you rich. Using this example, if you are 40 and invest $10,000 once and reinvest the dividends and stay in the stock market at all times, you have a chance of turning that money into a third of a million dollars at age 65. There's only one problem with this strategy: it leaves you time to do things you'd rather not do, like weeding the lawn or cleaning out the garage! For me, it leaves time to have breakfast once a week with the men at Millie's and I do so love the French toast.

LESSON 16
The Trolley Car
Never Be a Lender

When I was a about 11 years old, we lived at the north end of the trolley line in Omaha, Nebraska. I used to ride the trolley car through downtown to the end of the line and come back. When the motorman got out to change the trolley poles, I hid behind the seat to save the return fare. For me, life was momentarily suspended as I read the oleomargarine ads and watched the city slide by for a dime. Today, a lot of people are riding a financial trolley car to nowhere, but it's costing them a lot more than a dime.

So it's no surprise that a 1996 *USA Today*/CNN/Gallup poll found that only about four of every ten people are taking active steps to save money and get ready for retirement. No wonder a typical baby boomer who visits a credit counseling service today is 41 years old, makes about $40,000 a year in a full-time job, and is swimming in debt with nine credit cards and almost a $20,000 revolving balance.

But, as I near retirement, I can attest to the fact that retirement is not a fantasy; it happens to everyone. The good news, of course, is that you're still alive if you reach retirement. The bad news is that if you don't put your financial house in order over the years and instead rely on the shrinking retirement benefits from employers and the government, you can plunge into poverty.

What I want to share with you in this lesson is that saving money for retirement is not enough; you have to know what to do with the money you've saved. Pause for a moment and reflect on how you've invested your money. Then, consider that to catch a ride on the trolley car that really builds wealth, you have to learn the difference between being a "lender" and being an "investor." And I can tell you that in my case, over the past 30 years, most of my wealth has come from being an investor, not a lender.

The first opportunity for individuals to lend money and earn interest income came in 1472, in what many people consider the oldest bank in the world, the *Monte dei Paschi di Siena* in Italy. For the first time, a bank introduced the idea of letting other people manage your money in return for a profit. In Renaissance times, bankers such as the Medicis and the Fuggers grew wealthy, but so did the people who saved and lent them money.

In America, before computers, the passbook savings account remained unchanged from the 1500s, except the bank used a typewriter and a rubber stamp while the folks at *Monte dei Paschi di Siena* used a quill pen. Today, when banks can transfer money at nearly the speed of light, computers have transformed the passbook saving account into a money market account, but it still works the same way it did in the Renaissance.

More than 100 years ago, a group of 24 stockbrokers gathered under a buttonwood tree and began to trade shares of stock. They signed the Buttonwood Accord that established the New York Stock Exchange and Americans discovered for the first time that they could not only lend their money to a bank and earn interest on fixed savings, but they could also buy a share of a company's stock, earn dividends, and make profits on the increased value of the stock. This new idea of investing in stocks introduced some risk, which passbook savers rarely had, but it held out the hope that the average person could build wealth faster by investing in equities than by lending their money to a bank.

In 1896, Charles Dow created the Dow Jones Industrial Average, which is today the most-watched indicator of the U.S. stock market. The average consisted of the closing prices of 12 stocks and the first average price of industrial stocks was 40.94. In 1928, the Dow Jones Industrial Average was expanded to include 30 stocks, and the stocks that make up the Dow have been updated 20 times since then.

Over the past 100 years, the rise in the Dow Jones Industrial Average has been like climbing a mountain, sometimes falling in a valley, but always recovering and continuing its upward climb, yet this mountain has no peak. In recent history, the increase in the Dow Industrials has been more like a climb up the side of a skyscraper. The Dow closed above 2,000 for the first time in 1987. It took only another four years for the Dow to close above 3,000; another four years to close above 4,000; and by the close of 1996, the Dow had soared to almost 6,500.

In spite of this spectacular rise of the Dow, the market did crash in 1921, 1929, 1974, 1987, and to a lesser extent, in 1996. Recently, the average growth stock fund fell more than 20 percent in the 1987 crash and nearly 17 percent in the five-month bear market of 1990. During those downdrafts, many people felt they would get killed if they stayed in stocks. But history tells us that those who stayed in the market over time did very well. Why? Stocks show a remarkable ability to recover from major disasters. Investors who bought stocks at the top of the wildly inflated market in 1929, and held them for several decades, made more money than they would have made had they jumped back into bonds or fixed savings. In July 1996, the stock market took a big dive and the Dow Industrials fell to about 5,400, but by the end of the year, the Dow had climbed back to around 6,500. Those who lost faith in the stock market's ability to recover, and were on the sidelines for even a short period, missed one of the biggest short-term rallies in history.

In recent years, one of the smartest moves has been to become an owner of a bank and invest in shares of bank stocks, rather than to lend banks money in a savings account. Warren Buffett learned this a long time ago, and the price of his stock in Wells Fargo Bank over the past five years (August 31, 1991 to September 10, 1996) soared a whopping 234 percent.

But the clearest distinction between lenders (those who lend money to a bank for a period of time in an insured certificate of deposit or a bond) and investors (those who invest in bank stocks or bank stock mutual funds) may have occurred over the past five years. I was one of the investors, and I said, "Make it come true, baby!" and it did. The reason for my joy? Several mutual funds that invest in bank and savings and loan stocks returned, with dividends reinvested, about 28 percent in 1996 compared to a 5 percent return on a one-year CD.

Before you continue to talk to the happy people who offer you federally insured 5 percent savings, consider this: I didn't begin investing in 1996. The annualized total returns for these bank stock mutual funds over the past three years was about 24 percent, and over the past five years, about 26 percent. That's like earning a 5 percent return at the bank for the next five years each year.

Courage is doing what it takes to build real wealth despite one's fears. You must be willing to take some risks as an investor if you are going to make enough money to overcome inflation and live reasonably well in retirement. From talking to thousands of longtime bank savers who lack confidence in the stock market, I realize it will take courage for them to change the way they put their extra money to work. I hope you have the courage to change from a lender to an investor, just like I did.

LESSON 17
The Hare and the Tortoise
Staying in the Market

You spilled food on your shirt, your palms are clammy, and as you glibly chat with a friend, your heart is suddenly pounding as you think about the hair-raising dive in the stock market and how much money you are losing. What's running through your mind is how to get out of the stock market and save what's left of your nest egg. You are afraid of looking dumb holding stocks in a market crash. I know it's much easier to weather the storm if you're 30 or 40, but whatever your age, you need to put the carnage behind you. As I told you in the last lesson, if you want to build a realistic retirement nest egg, you have to marry the stock market as soon as you can and stick with it for the rest of your life.

"You should be able to double your money in the stock market in about five years, in a 5 percent CD in 15 years."

The way most people invest their money today reminds me of an Aesop fable. The hares think they can do better if they're constantly on the move, always looking for the new investment to buy or an old one to sell as they race toward the finish line. The tortoises believe they don't need to zig or zag; instead they hold on to what they have and make steady progress toward a goal. If the going gets rough, they pull into their shell, but they never give up. Imagine what it would be like if investors were like tortoises. Investing in the stock market would be a cinch. They would simply invest and stay the course. Bad news would bounce off their shell and good news would brighten their day. I don't know what good it will do to tell most people simply to sit on their hands when the market takes an occasional hair-raising dive and wait for it to recover and make them rich, but that's exactly what I'm going to tell anyone reading this book.

I remember the first time I ignored the stock market and stayed the course. I couldn't believe the money I was making doing nothing. Just 15 years ago, starting in 1980, the Dow Jones Industrial Average was around 800. Fifteen years later, at the start of 1995, the Dow was at about 4,000. Then the Dow sprinted from 4,000 to 5,000 from February to November of that year. By the end of 1996, the frenzied pace of the stock market shot the Dow up to 6,500. Of course, at these heights, moving from one 1,000 milestone to another gets easier and easier because each point is less on a percentage basis.

I don't recommend that you shovel *all* your money into stocks, but if you had opened an individual retirement account in 1980 and invested $2,000 in a Standard & Poor's 500 stock index fund, then reinvested the dividends and kept your hands off your money over the succeeding 15 years, by 1995 your $2,000 could have grown to around $16,000.

Then there are the scrooges who take no risk. They would have invested the same $2,000 a year in a bank certificate of deposit paying 5 percent interest, and 15 years later it would have been worth about $4,150.

I think the lesson is clear: *Where* you invest makes all the difference in how your retire. If you are investing long-term for retirement or to pay for a child's college education, forget about being a scrooge who takes no risks and plays it safe with fixed savings, money market accounts or money market funds. Why? Those strategies are the financial equivalents of shooting yourself in the foot. If I had a blackboard, I'd write this on it: "You should be able to double your money in about five years in the stock market and in about 15 years with fixed savings or an insured certificate of deposit."

There are, however, no guarantees in the stock market. What goes up sometimes comes down. The market's history of major dips has not been forgotten, despite today's seemingly unsinkable stock market, and someday history will repeat itself and stocks will once again take a beating. In fact, the stock market may not give you an average 15 percent annual return as it has done since the 1980s, but history tells us that investing in stock funds is a heck of a lot smarter than lending your money to a bank.

I know this sounds crazy to a lot of people and probably heresy to a banker, but if you want to build wealth, you must invest in a growing America. It has worked for me over the years and I have no reason to believe it won't work for you in the future.

LESSON 18
Sitting on Your Hands
Long-Term Savings in the Market

This lesson is so important that I'm going to tell you once again why so many investors lose money in the stock market. The majority of my wisdom comes from my own experience. I like to think it's like wearing old shoes. After my feet get comfortable in a pair of shoes, I keep them until they fall apart. As long as they feel and look good why throw them away? This drives my wife nuts. She has a closet full of shoes, and she buys new ones all the time. But I don't care. To me, keeping old comfortable shoes is a lot like keeping my investments in the stock market. I know it works and there is no need to try something new.

That's because Wall Street, like a giant casino, is in reality a game of pure chance. The problem is that no one in the casino or in the stock market knows in advance when to buy, sell, bet on the future, or when to stay on the sidelines. One of the oldest sayings on "the Street" is that "the market has a mind of its own." That's why it's important, after you invest in good stock mutual funds, to stay in the market at all times. Why? Because by selling stock or stock funds to get out of a down market, investors invariably fail to get back in before the next bull market begins. Unless their investments are in an individual retirement account or other retirement plan, the tax system also works against the buy-and-sell trader. If they sell, they must pay taxes on the appreciation they've built up in their funds at the time of sale. This applies to any fund, even if they switch funds within a family of funds. If they take a loss (inside an IRA or other retirement plan you can't deduct an investment loss), they can only write off $3,000 a year against those losses.

Warren Buffett, who was, according to *Forbes* magazine, the second richest person in the world in 1996, learned this lesson early in life. He simply invested in good growth companies like Coca-Cola, Gillette, Disney, McDonald's, and Wells Fargo Bank, and waited for the companies' stock to make him rich.

Andrew Kilpatrick, author of *Permanent Value: The Story of Warren Buffett*, published by AKPE in 1996, wrote that "if you handed Warren Buffett $10,000 in 1956, today it would be worth about $140 million, and that figure is after all taxes, fees, and expenses. That would be a 14,000-fold return on his money in an era when the Dow Jones Industrial Average rose about tenfold. Even if you arrived late at the party and did not invest in Berkshire Hathaway until 1965 when Buffett took it over, a $10,000 investment then would now be worth about $30 million.

"One problem with Buffett/Berkshire's buy low, don't sell story," says Kilpatrick, "is that it seems unbelievable. People are skeptical because most investors have trouble just treading water. Therefore, it's hard to relate to making millions upon millions of dollars."

Still convinced that you can "beat the market" by jumping in and out of it and constantly paying taxes on your profits? Well, in all my years of experience, I've never met anyone who could consistently, year in and year out, beat the market average by knowing just when to buy and sell. You may become the first person, but until that happens, I'm going to believe it's not possible.

I don't think I'm wrong in this case. Besides, I have history on my side. A study by the University of Michigan's School of Business found that if investors were out of the market and missed the 90 best days between 1963 and 1993, they would have lost 95 percent of the market's gains. If they invested $1,000 in 1963 and stayed in the market continuously to 1993, they'd have $24,300. With the same investment, jumping in and out and missing the 90 best days in the past 30 years, they'd have only $2,100, even less than with passbook savings rates.

Let's look at a recent period. During the decade of the 1980s, there were 2,528 trading days on Wall Street. Based on the Standard & Poor's 500 stock index, if you stayed in the stock market at all times and reinvested your dividends, your annualized return would have been about 17.5 percent. But if you were out of the market for only *the 40 best days* of the decade, your annualized return would have been just 3.9 percent.

On the other hand, if you ignored Wall Street and were a "standpatter" over the past 25 years, buying and holding blue chip stocks like Philip Morris, McDonald's, Pepsico, Coca-Cola, and Gillette, you would have posted an average annual total return of more than 16 percent. At that rate, an investor could have more than doubled his or her money every five years. Just $10,000 invested 25 years ago could now be worth about $350,000.

Remember, the most important thing you have to do to build wealth is to invest in America's growth companies. The hardest part is finding the willpower to do this when it gets really scary, when the stock market falls like a rock. But Wall Street history tells us that's the best time to stay in the market.

This lesson tells us that those who ignore the fireworks on Wall Street are the real winners. You're not likely to make a quick buck by investing in the latest mutual fund fad or by trying to buy or sell at just the right time, but you're sure to build a hefty retirement nest egg by simply following Warren Buffett's advice: Invest in high-quality stocks and sit on your hands.

LESSON 19
Small Beginnings
Earning Money on Money You've Invested

Every year, just outside our kitchen window in a large bush, my wife and I watch a bird build a nest. Judging by our bird book, we think it's a golden-crowned sparrow and its plaintive, whistled notes—*oh dear me*—fill our kitchen with its song each day. As I watch this hardworking nest builder, I realize that it's a tough job building a nest with only a beak and feet to work with. The bird puts one twig after another on the nest until it has completed the job. Wind and rain never stand in its way, and I sometimes wonder, as it looks at us through the window, if it thinks of us as lazy. But in the end, there is a nest full of eggs and life starts all over again.

Building a retirement nest egg requires the same determination: you gather one dollar at a time and constantly shore up your nest. But, like the untended nest outside our kitchen window each fall, the untended retirement nest egg will crumble unless it is continually patched up with new dollars.

Unlike the hardworking bird, however, you have unseen helping hands that can make your nest egg grow so large it could eventually take over the entire bush. These helping hands are called "compounding," or your ability over time to make money on the money you've *already* saved and invested. This method of building wealth was not overlooked by the first American identified in print as a "millionaire," Pierre Lorillard in 1843. Nor was it forgotten by the first person to be written up as a "billionaire," John D. Rockefeller in 1861.

Yet, most people today fail to understand that it is primarily through compounding that people get rich.

The point of this lesson is that the magic of compounding takes time. The testimony to the tremendous power of compounding over time is that if you invested just $100 in the Dow Jones Industrials in 1900, you would now have more than $61 million! True, you can't get rich overnight, but compounding can make you rich if you start to invest early and continue over time. That's because, from a practical point of view, most people will find that from 80 percent to more than 90 percent of the assets in their ultimate retirement nest egg will come from money *they never saved or invested in the first place!*

Let's go over this lesson one more time so you can see the important points to remember. Let's say a young man and woman start to build their respective nest eggs at age 30 by putting $2.74 a day ($1,000 a year) into good stock funds in an individual retirement account or company retirement plan. It is easy to do this via an automatic withdrawal from each paycheck.

At age 65, they will have contributed only $35,000 to those retirement nest eggs, yet the final amount in each account can equal $1 million. Now we are close to the lucky stiff who won the lottery. Investing just $35,000 equals $1 million at retirement. But what if these people waited just five years—until age 35—to begin socking away $2.74 a day? At age 65, they each would have invested $30,000, but their nest eggs could amount to only about half a million dollars. Waiting until age 40, with the same annual contributions, there would be a $25,000 investment by age 65, but it could be worth only $250,000. But even starting at age 40, the nest egg consisted of 90 percent of money earned through compounding and just 10 percent of money invested.

For another lesson in the magic of compounding, consider the tale of two young people: The first one is age 19. He earns at least $2,000 a year and with the help of the parents puts $2,000 into his individual retirement account and does this for just the next eight years, to age 26. With a return of 10 percent each year (income plus growth), at age 65, he could have over $1 million in an individual retirement account on an eight-year investment of just $16,000. But the magic of compounding can be cruel. If the second person waits just eight years later—to age 27—to start individual retirement account contributions, he will have to make a $2,000 annual contribution *for the next 39 years,* or a total of $78,000, and the results at age 65 could be only about $800,000.

Like the bird outside our kitchen window, you need to bring "dollar twigs" to your nest on a regular basis. For many people, one of the best ways to do this is called dollar cost averaging. This refers to the practice of buying shares of stock or mutual funds on a monthly basis instead of all at once. Because you buy stock or funds at different prices over time, you tend to average out the cost. That way, you don't have to try to outguess the market or waste time trying to find the perfect moment to jump in because dollar cost averaging is as close as you can come to infallible investing. And, for many people, dollar cost averaging forces them to save and invest regularly, to "pay themselves first" with automatic withdrawals from their checking account.

Let's suppose you invest $100 a month in the ABC fund. In the first month, if ABC shares are selling at $10, you'd buy ten shares. If the price falls to $5 a share in the next month, you'd buy 20 shares. The following month, ABC fund's share price might climb back to $7.50 a share, and you'd buy about 13.3 shares. Then in the fourth month, ABC share's might soar to $12.50 a share, and you'd buy eight shares. Over this four-month period, you would have invested a total of $400 and purchased about 51.3 shares, at an average share price of $7.80.

While this is only an example to illustrate how dollar cost averaging works, there are times when you can wind up owning more shares with dollar cost averaging than if you bought the shares only when the market, and the share price, were rising. A friend of mine says he likes dollar cost averaging because when share prices are low, he can buy more shares, and when they are expensive, he buys fewer shares. Like all investment techniques, dollar cost averaging does not guarantee you a profit. But, if you sell at the bottom of a market, no system is going to give you a gain.

I should make it clear right now that I sincerely believe everything I've just told you. No matter where you live, no matter how much you make, if you follow this lesson's advice, learn to spend less than you earn over the years, and invest regularly, you can retire wealthy. I don't know what you're waiting for, except maybe you don't think this plan will work. But compounding worked for Lorillard and Rockefeller and it did for me, and there's no reason to think it won't work for you.

LESSON 20
The Trip to Retirement
Turn $5,000 into $20 Million

In many ways, building a retirement fund or saving for college is a lot like driving a car on the freeway. You have several exits en route to your destination and often only one will get you where you want to go. You can take the first one that comes along, spend all your money, and wonder why life continues to end up in a dead-end street. Or, you can pull off the freeway, smell the flowers, and wait for something to happen. Maybe the phone will ring and you'll hear, "Hello, I want to tell you your Uncle Henry just died and left you $5 million."

Experience, however, tells me that if you want to build wealth, you must do it yourself unless you have an Uncle Henry somewhere in your family tree. It's like finding the right exit on the freeway of life and heading for it with all the willpower you can command.

Because I've seen so many people wait for an Uncle Henry–type phone call, or for a lotto ticket to hit pay dirt with $10 million, *I want to restate this lesson again:* Sudden wealth doesn't happen overnight. This statement might have whizzed right by you the last time I told you, but even if you are middle-aged, haven't read a book since *The Cat in the Hat,* and break into a sweat just thinking about investing your money, all is not lost.

I told you that if you invest $10,000 in good-quality stock funds, based on the recent history of Wall Street, you could have about $20,000 in five years if you leave the investment alone and reinvest the dividends. I've also said that your investment in good stock funds could double every five years, as it has for me in the past, and in ten years without any more investments, your nest egg could be worth about $40,000. Give it another five years and the amount could top $80,000. After 20 years your $10,000 original investment could turn into a cash windfall of about $160,000. There are no guarantees, of course, and the stock market may not continue an upward climb at its recent pace, but all of our investing is based on the rearview mirror concept. We can clearly see the past, but no one I've met on Wall Street has been able to see correctly into the future.

But what about spending the money in retirement? Chances are you won't need all the money in the first five years. So if you can leave your stock fund investments alone, in the next five years your nest egg could double again to $320,000. The good news is that the money machine you've built up during your working years just keeps on working like some perpetual-motion machine. The $160,000 growth in your nest egg over the first five years in retirement works out to an annual increase of $32,000. Not bad when you consider that just 25 years earlier you invested only $10,000. But, even if you take out part of the assets each year to live on, your money machine will still provide you with financial security while you collect your meager Social Security benefits.

I call this method of leaving money alone my "times two" money. That's because the simple math of investing in good stock mutual funds tells me that over the past decade or more, the average annual stock fund's total return, with dividends reinvested, was about 15 percent a year. At this rate,

I should be able to turn $10,000 into $20,000 in five years without investing any new money. Compare this return to a $10,000 investment in a fixed savings account earning 5 percent. Ignoring yearly taxes on interest income, the compounded value after five years is only $12,763. How strange. If inflation ran 4 percent a year during this five-year period, it would take $12,200 to equal the purchasing power of $10,000 today. In a silly world of making money with a savings account, your future purchasing power could stand still.

Fortunately for me and my kids, the lighting bolt hit home when I discovered that I might be able to double my money every five years in the stock market, compared to every 15 years with a fixed savings account.

LESSON 21
The Magic of Hype
Mutual Fund Ratings

Because my father was born in Denmark, I've traveled there several times looking for my roots. But finding one's roots can often be a difficult task. In his hometown of Odense, I found Hans Christian Andersen's home, but in the phone book I found 15 pages of phone numbers for Jorgensens. The name was everywhere I went, but I never found my dad's home. In Copenhagen, I did find the Little Mermaid. It actually exists, sitting on a rock waiting for a ship to pass.

That's more than you can say about the reality of the claims made by mutual funds regarding their performance. The truly remarkable thing is that people don't understand how funds figure their returns. They invest simply on the basis of hype and past history, somehow hoping that lightning will strike again where it did before.

It sometimes seems that almost every fund you read about is ranked number one in past performance. But those advertised rankings can be from unrelated categories and may leave out a lot of other funds with better performance records. Or a fund may rank itself with only a few other funds of its size and select a time period when it did especially well. Fund regulators consider this practice of comparing just the right performance numbers akin to a shell game where the real performance is hidden under one of the cups.

To achieve the best performance numbers, some funds act like a barker at a carnival who promotes incredible acts that are all behind closed doors. These funds don't even show their own performance record, but use an index as a proxy. They compare what you could have earned in the entire stock market while playing down the fund's actual performance, or even omitting it. Yet another way some funds avoid the truth is to neglect to mention their sales commissions. Without factoring in this drag on performance, the fund's return looks a lot better to would-be investors. What does all this mean? Not much. At any given time, about 650 different mutual funds can be ranked number one.

Mutual fund performance is based on "total return." This is figured by taking the value of the shares at the beginning of a period, plus any dividend payouts, and plus or minus the change in the value of the shares at the end of the period. For example, if your stock fund's shares were worth $1,000 a year ago, and the value of the shares including any dividends and capital gains increases to $1,250 a year later, your total return for one year would be 25 percent. On the other hand, if the value of the shares a year later was only $900, including any dividends, your total return would be –10 percent.

What you often see in magazine and newspaper advertisements are a fund's one-year total return (over the past 12 months, not what investors have been earning in the current year) and the fund's average annual total return since the inception of the fund. The numbers may look great in the ad, but the past returns are good news only for the people who owned the fund in the past. No one can ever be positively sure they'll get the same results in the future.

When a fund did well the previous year, its ads tout that year's total returns. The fund's current year returns may be lousy, but they're often not mentioned or they're hidden in the fine print. For example, if you invest in a bond mutual fund with a previous 12-month total return of 12 percent, you'll have no idea what you'll earn in the next 12 months. The ads look good and you're sitting there with a 5 percent CD, so you say to yourself that 12 percent sounds like a good deal. But interest rates may have taken a big fall during the previous year and the fund could have made hefty profits on the increased prices of the bonds in its portfolio. Now, however, after you invest, interest rates may be rising and the fund's total return over the next 12 months could be only 3 percent.

When I invest, I look for a fund that has had great total returns for the past one, five, and even ten years. I've found that the chances are good that a stock fund that has delivered above-average total returns over such a long period will continue to do so in the future.

Before you fall asleep with big profits dancing in your head, remember that if you invest in the number one fund this year, all you'll get is the past history of that fund. This doesn't mean that ratings don't count, but before you invest, you need to check out just how the fund got its performance rating, how many funds were in the comparison group, and over how long the results were based. Otherwise you're just fishing in the dark, hoping that a big one will bite.

LESSON 22
The Dance Is Never Over
When to Invest in Stocks

"Any time is a good time to invest in the stock market."

If Cinderella were dancing on Wall Street, she would know that the clock never strikes midnight. She would also know that any time she had some spare money would be a good time to invest in the stock market. And Cinderella would be right. But apparently, most people never met Cinderella at the ball because they believe that it's important to wait for just the right time to invest in stocks. But it's not important. If you put money into the stock market whenever you have some spare cash rather than waiting for just the right time, you'll get better results nearly two-thirds of the time. Whether the stock market is breaking new records or laying an egg, *today is still the best time to invest.*

My father told me to invest in stocks every time I had some spare cash and forget about what people say the stock market will do, and it was one of the best pieces of advice he gave me. It cut my level of anxiety when I continued to invest in a falling stock market and it gave me the courage to continue investing when everyone else said I was crazy. It turned out my father was right. When I was growing up, he was already right. Around our house, Rule #1 was my dad was always right. When he's wrong, Rule #2 was to refer back to Rule #1. Well, in this case, I didn't need to use Rule #2.

Let's say you were a soothsayer with investment newsletters spread across your desk and you made a $5,000 investment in stocks each year for the past 20 years at the best possible time each year, when the market was at its low point for the year. Now let's say that I, following my father's advice to invest my money when I could, made the same $5,000 annual investment at the worst possible time each year, when the stock market was at its highest point. How would our results compare? Get ready for a surprise. If you could have picked the very best time each year to invest, you would have only ended up with less than 2 percent more than I did.

Wall Street is littered with banana peels for people who can't make up their mind on the best time to invest. Each time they wait, the market runs away from them. Only ten years ago the Dow Jones Industrial Average first hit 2,000. Was that a good time to invest? If you said no, you probably kicked yourself in the pants when, five years later, the Dow surpassed 3,000. Still not a good time to invest? Maybe you became paranoid and suspicious of the fireworks on Wall Street and sat on your hands. In 1996, the Dow climbed through 5,500 and finished the year around 6,500 and many experts predict the Dow will top 10,000 by the turn of the century.

So you see, Wall Street is really like the ball with Cinderella. But, unlike Cinderella, whose ball gown turned back into rags at midnight, you have an opportunity every day to invest, and each day you wait you stand a good chance of missing the party as the stock market continues to climb.

LESSON 23
The Magic Ingredient
Asset Allocation

There are only five things you can do with your money: You can give it away, spend it, lend it to someone else, invest it, and pay your taxes. What you do with your money is, of course, your own business, but if you really want to build wealth, the only one of these that counts is the part you invest. You probably learned this in the eighth grade, but I just want to repeat it here because most people only spend their money and pay their taxes.

"Asset allocation can account for as much as 94 percent of your future financial gains."

This seems like a good time to talk about what to do with the money you've put aside to invest. First, ignore all the fancy advertisements for the next "hot" stock or mutual fund, tune out the "talking heads" on television and their advice on where the market is going and what to buy, and forget what the papers say about the Federal Reserve Board hiking interest rates. What's really important to your long-term financial health is how you allocate your money.

I've already told you that my wife says I can't buy the right style of clothes. I like cuffs on my pants. "They're out," she says. I like to wear long-sleeved shirts all year. "They're out in the summer," she tells me. But even *I* know enough not to buy 40 yellow shirts. Yet many people are perfectly content to keep their investment dollars entirely in a single type of investment, which is like buying 40 yellow shirts. Luckily, you don't need a crystal ball to know what to do with your savings and investments. What's really important is something called *asset allocation*. I call it the "big enchilada" because nothing is more important in building wealth than allocating your assets, or spreading out your investments in various ways.

Of all the lessons in this book, the most important to your future financial security could be asset allocation. If you can accept that fact then you've taken a giant step toward improving your bottom line. Let me put it another way: Trying to get wealthy without asset allocation is like trying to bake a cake without flour. I never made that mistake, but after 40 years of marriage, I rarely ever bake a cake. My job is to lick the beaters and my favorite frosting is chocolate.

The classic description of asset allocation is the process of developing a diversified investment portfolio by mixing different assets in varying proportions. Or, in simple English, don't put all your eggs in one basket. How you allocate your assets will depend on your age, your need for monthly income, and your risk tolerance. Therefore, no one asset allocation plan works for everyone. But, before you allocate your assets and plan to head for a beachfront paradise in retirement, don't overlook your first step: Set aside enough cash to cover three to six months of living expenses, or for other emergencies.

Then, remember an easy rule of thumb to use in your asset allocation. You simply put at least 100 minus your age in stock mutual funds. Using this formula, the older you are, the less you have in equities and the more you have in income-producing bonds. Let's say, for example, you are age 40. Then, at least 60 percent of your long-term investments should be in the stock market or stock mutual funds. The balance of your assets at age 40 could be invested 30 percent in bonds and 10 percent in cash or fixed savings accounts. In individual or company-sponsored retirement plans, however, almost all of the money earned during your working life should be in stock mutual funds.

The basic asset allocation plan often used on Wall Street to explain how to develop a diversified portfolio is called the "robotic approach." It says to put 55 percent of your assets in stocks, 35 percent in bonds, and 10 percent in cash-equivalent savings accounts. If you stick to this fixed blend, you will consistently take some profits from the winning assets and make up for the assets that have performed poorly.

If you want to fine-tune your asset allocation, you might select one of the following *long-term* portfolios:

- Relatively conservative, income-oriented, in or near retirement. Put 45 percent of your assets in stocks, 35 percent in bonds, and 20 percent in cash or short-term savings accounts.
- A moderate approach for middle-of-the-roaders between the ages of 45 and 65. Put 60 percent in stocks, 35 percent in bonds, and 5 percent in cash.
- An aggressive approach for those under age 45. For a growth-oriented portfolio with little or no income, put 85 percent in stocks, 10 percent in bonds, and 5 percent in cash.
- A more aggressive approach for those under age 35. Put 95 percent in stocks and 5 percent in bonds.

Why should you remember this golden rule of asset allocation? Because after almost four decades of financial planning, I know it can often make the difference between just getting by in retirement and living a life on the golf course. Remember, when *asset allocation can account for as much as 94 percent of your future gains,* you know you've struck pay dirt.

If this sounds a bit weird, consider this: Studies have shown that only slightly more than 2 percent of your future gains can come from your individual stock and bond selections, less than 2 percent from market timing (knowing when to buy and sell stocks and funds), and about 2 percent from all other factors.

Authors Gary Brinson, L. Randolph Hood, and Gilbert Beebower wrote an extraordinary article in the July–August 1986 issue of *Financial Analysts Journal.* They examined the performance of 91 large pension plans over three-year periods between 1974 and 1983. When they developed a way to measure the impact of investment decisions, they found that 93.6 percent of these pension plans' performance was explained by their investment policy (or asset allocation). Only 6.4 percent resulted from the ability of the pension fund managers to time the market or pick the best securities.

Private, noninsured pension funds in 1993, according to the Federal Reserve Board, had allocated their investments somewhere around 50 percent in stocks, 20 percent in U.S. government bonds, 15 percent in corporate bonds, about 10 percent in demand and time deposits, and about 5 percent in money market funds.

Now I just want to see if you have been paying attention to all of this, because chances are you have not. Like most American households invested in mutual funds, you have probably overlooked the magic of asset allocation and how important investing in equities can become to your financial future. According to the Investment Company Institute, in 1996 only 23 percent of all households had invested in stock funds.

As I write this, my mind is churning. Why can't people realize that, over time, asset allocation can account for as much as 94 percent of their future gains? One reason that some fast-talking brokers and financial planners don't tell you this is because they want you to believe that no matter how your assets are allocated, they know how to find just the right stock or bond that will put you on easy street. But even if they are good stock pickers (and most of the time they aren't), their insight and timing will probably account (according to the studies on asset allocation) for no more than about 2 percent of your future gains.

The most important point in this lesson is to realize that how you allocate your investments in stocks, bonds, and savings accounts is far more important than what and when you buy or sell along the way. If you are fascinated by all of this, you should be. And maybe the dance on Wall Street will come into better focus when you realize that it's easy to allocate your assets.

LESSON 24
Rolling a Stone
The Effects of Inflation

The mythological Greek figure Sisyphus was condemned to Hades with the fate of repeatedly rolling a huge stone up a hill, only to have it roll down again each time. People who earn interest income in an attempt to save for retirement or college expenses also struggle mightily, like Sisyphus, to keep an enormous stone from rolling back over them and flattening their money.

Even more mythological than Sisyphus is the notion that you can build a retirement fund or save for college costs over time with EE savings bonds, money market accounts, or fixed savings accounts. For the most part, your net after-tax annual interest income will barely keep up with the rate of inflation, and when you later spend your money, you could have no more purchasing power than when you started putting money aside.

The myth that you can save for the long-term with short-term savings accounts is perpetuated by the institutions that want your money. In fact, they can't wait for you to rush in the door, fill out the papers, deposit your money, pick up your free gifts, and hit the street. While you're being "nickeled-and-dimed" to death for every bank or savings and loan service, the bank has already wired your money to New York where it will earn a lot more money on your deposit than it pays you.

There was a time when passbook savings meant real wealth. Most readers are probably too young to remember earning interest income before inflation and the advent of computers. In the days of my youth, a bank teller would list my deposits and withdrawals in my passbook, initial the transaction, and use a rubber stamp for the date. Clutching my passbook in my hands, I left the bank each time I made a deposit with a feeling of security, and if I knew someone who had numbers in their passbook over $1,000, I though of that as real wealth.

But today you can no longer build wealth with a passbook savings account. You lend your money in return for interest payments and the bank guarantees the repayment of your money with the help of federal deposit insurance, so you may feel you have avoided risk. But lending money long-term in a savings account is one of the biggest risks you can take!

It may not matter to you that the price tag for a Rolls-Royce Corniche IV convertible jumped 5.6 percent in one year to $284,000, or that imported chocolate truffles have increased 9.5 percent a year recently, but it will matter to you what you pay for college costs, groceries, car insurance and medical care in the years to come. That's because *money is worth only what it will buy when you want to spend it.*

My mother tells me that she can remember when a quart of milk cost 10 cents and the milkman came by the house with a horse and wagon. I still remember the red five-cent Coke machines with the bottles surrounded by ice water. But today, thinking of my youth, it's often hard for me to realize just how much more everything costs today. When my wife and I were going through one of the seemingly endless number of gift shops in the California wine country, she asked me to get her a soft drink. Eager to escape the gift shops, I asked the man behind the deli counter for a small Coke. I confidently laid a dollar bill on the counter. After all, the soft drink in the paper cup was mostly ice. As I reached for the Coke, I was told that I had to put more money on the counter. How in the world, I wondered, could a small Coke in a paper cup filled with ice cost more than a dollar?

But inflation creeps up on us slowly. In 1969, when I bought my first new Cadillac, it cost $5,936. If you were rich then and had a $100,000 certificate of deposit yielding 7 percent, your annual interest income could buy the Cadillac and you would have enough left over for a holiday cruise. Today, the interest from that same CD wouldn't even make the down payment on a new $42,000 Cadillac, and you can forget about the cruise.

Let's say that in the future, inflation is about 4 percent a year. After a decade of 4 percent inflation, a basket of goods that cost $1,000 today would cost $1,480. In just 15 years, at the same rate of inflation, your $1,000 would need to grow to $1,800 just to keep up with inflation. In 20 years it would need to grow to $2,190, or double your $1,000 today. The bottom line is that you have to earn after-tax investment returns that more than beat inflation before you can even think about building wealth and living better.

To put this in perspective, if inflation runs 4 percent a year over the next 20 years, here's how much some familiar items could cost in the year 2017:

	1997	*2017*
Big Mac with fries	$ 4.25	$ 9.30
Man's suit	225.00	492.75
Lunch at work	6.00	13.15
New car, average	21,000.00	46,000.00
Dinner out for two	65.00	142.35

To be able to afford these soaring prices, it's easy to see you'll need to earn a hefty after-tax return on your investments in the years ahead. But can you with fixed savings? Not likely. To see how your savings can be overtaken by inflation, grab a paper and pencil and follow me on the road to poverty. Assume you can earn 5 percent on an insured certificate of deposit. After all, you tell yourself, it's safe, it's easy to understand, and 5 percent is a lot better than a money market account. In theory this may sound great, but in practice it isn't. The problem is that if you're in a high tax bracket, you're only keeping about 3 percent of the

5 percent you earn on savings after taxes. It's like being on a treadmill at a gym and you're always running slower than the moving belt.

But now the treadmill really speeds up. To figure your future purchasing power, you also need to account for inflation. If today you make a one-time deposit of $1,000 in fixed savings, and if inflation ran 4 percent a year during the next ten years, you'd need $1,480 to match the purchasing power you have now. If you continued to net 3 percent after taxes each year, your net savings in ten years would amount to only $1,340. Your spendable cash in the future would not even keep up with inflation. As far as building any real wealth, forget about it.

Well, so what's all this to you? If you can't earn enough money after taxes and inflation to build wealth, the whole idea of financial planning is a myth. Let's look at a real-life example. In the last 12 years, the average price of a new car and truck has risen from about $11,500 in 1984 to about $21,800 in 1996. That's about a 90 percent hike in the showroom price. Now let's say you have figured out a way to earn 5 percent a year on your money *after* taxes and you started saving in 1984. If you saved $625 at the beginning of each year, you'd have about $10,500 by the start of 1996. But that amount would only equal the increase in the price of the car over that period and you would have saved nothing toward the purchase of the car.

As for money market accounts, consider them to be valet parking. You call and someone will bring your money. When you don't need the money, you park it to earn interest. But investors who use money market accounts for long-term savings will find that our metaphorical treadmill is truly racing out of control. Take your pencil again and follow me. If you're earning 3.5 percent in a money market account and you're in a combined federal and state tax bracket of only 20 percent, your after-tax annual return is only 2.8 percent. Again, assuming a 4 percent annual inflation rate, you are now building spendable cash at a rate far less than the rising prices of the goods and services you will buy later on.

But fixed savings do have a place for short-term savings goals, emergencies, and for ready cash. For such purposes, I use two different kinds of accounts. One is a no-load ultra-short-term bond mutual fund with a portfolio that averages about ten months to maturity, compared to three months to maturity for a true money market account or money market fund. With its short-term maturities, this "almost a money market fund" has minimum share price fluctuation and risk, and for the past five years, its average annual total return has been 7.4 percent. The fund has free check writing (each check must be for over $500), so I can tap my money any time I want.

The other account I have for ready cash is a no-load tax-free municipal bond fund. The fund comes with preprinted checks (minimum $500 for each check) to access the money. Because I live in California, and the state has a state income tax, I invest in a "single-state" fund that exempts both federal and state income taxes. If you live in a state with a state income tax, look for a single-state fund that invests only in bonds within your state. If your state has no state income taxes (Alaska, Florida, South Dakota, Texas, Washington, and Wyoming), you can shop for "national" tax-free funds that are free of only federal income taxes.

How much difference does it make to save tax-free compared to a fully taxable savings account if you're in a 30 percent combined federal and state tax bracket? It's like a jogger trying to outrun someone on a bicycle. Over the past five years, my municipal income bond fund has returned, on average, about 5 percent tax-free a year. For most people, that's like trying to find a taxable savings account paying more than 7 percent.

To find out whether a tax-free investment makes sense for you, compare its taxable equivalent yield to the yield on a taxable investment with a similar maturity, using this simple calculation:

Divide the tax-free yield (in this case 5 percent) by one minus your tax bracket (in the above example, 30 percent). One minus 0.30 equals 0.70. If you then divide 5 percent by 0.70, the answer is 7.14 percent. That's what you'd need to earn on a taxable account to equal a 5 percent tax-free yield.

If earning a tax-equivalent yield of well over 7 percent sounds a bit absurd, consider this: Each year, on average, the tax-free bond fund has also returned 3 percent in capital gains. Because the capital gains are taxable (only interest income is tax-free), I've been earning a tax-equivalent return of some 10 percent a year, or more than three times the return of a typical taxable 3 percent money market account.

The point of this lesson is that using a savings account or money market account to save for college or to build a retirement nest egg is like trying to fill the Grand Canyon with a garden hose. You'll get the ground wet but not much more. And while you appear to be playing it safe, you're actually running an enormous risk that you'll have less purchasing power in the future than you have today.

LESSON 25
Clipped Wings
Too Eager to Invest

If you want a bird to remain in an open cage, you clip its wings. The bird doesn't know this and it tries to fly, but its wings can't lift its body off the ground. A brokerage term for someone who is willing and eager to fly into any investment that's not likely to get off the ground is a "clipped-winger."

Since President Reagan gave us financial deregulation and the brokers and mutual funds put their computers to work, a slew of new products have hit the street and their numbers continue to multiply each month. Existing products are also continually being shuffled, rearranged, and combined to form a dizzying array of new opportunities. Almost before the ink has dried on the ad copy for another new "can't miss" investment, people are waiting for another chance to have their financial wings clipped. Trying to make money from this confusing mess can be absolutely exasperating.

Believe me, I know about exasperation. Sometimes I like to go out in the evening to a movie or a play; my wife likes to stay home and watch television. I have no control over this, but I've learned not to make the woman in my life angry and, judging from the reviews of many of the current movies and plays, she may be right after all.

With the ever-increasing number of new ways to make and lose money, my rule of thumb is never invest in something you don't fully understand. Before you trust your money to someone else, the first question you should ask is what are my chances that I'll get my money back? Then, be sure to check out where your money is supposed to be invested, how this investment vehicle is expected to work, and if the projected return is realistic. Next, find out the maximum you can lose if the market goes against you and what it will cost you to get your money back if your plans change. And last, don't even flap your wings at any special investment "opportunity" until you learn why *you've* been asked to invest in it.

Here are several ways some clipped-wingers invested their money without asking these questions.

A reader of my newsletter wrote me, "I invested $15,000 in a limited partnership through our financial adviser. He's left the company and we can't get any response from the general partners who have since moved to the Virgin Islands. I can't get any reply to my calls and letters and I can't find out what the investment is worth or file my taxes. What can I do?"

A woman who worked in an attorney's office had built up her savings to a hefty sum, when she was talked into investing much of it in a tax-deferred annuity. After less than two years, her mother became ill and she needed some of the money to pay expenses and for additional income. Only then did she find out that if she withdrew her money from the annuity it would cost her much of what she had worked a lifetime to accumulate. She told me that if she took any money out of the annuity, she'd face a 10 percent IRS penalty for early withdrawal, a 9 percent annuity surrender charge, and taxes on every penny of income. Two years after she had flapped her wings and rushed into a "can't miss" way to invest, she lost more than 20 percent of her investment.

"I invested $62,000 for my 73-year-old mother with a broker in a U.S. Government Securities fund," another letter began. "The value has now dropped to just over $51,000. We told the broker we wanted preservation of principal and a monthly income check. My mother, at her age, can't replace her financial security. We picked the most conservative, 100 percent government-backed fund and she has lost over 17 percent. When I point-blank asked the broker what he thought, he said he could eventually see my mother's money getting back to the $57,000 range."

Before you make the same mistakes, follow me with this fable. Once upon a time, a weary traveler stopped by the side of the road. With the big changes in personal finance, he knew he had to learn how to manage his money better.

Then along came a man with his arms full of books and magazines on personal finance. He said to the weary traveler, "I can help you learn what you need to know *before* you invest and it can save you a lot of money and worry about your investments."

"But you'll charge me some money for this help," the traveler said.

"My purse is near empty," said the man. "I must pay the printer and my rent."

"I'll think about it," said the traveler. "It might cost me some money to learn what I need to know to manage my money."

So the man with the books and magazines went on his way. After a time another man came along from the banks, brokers, and financial planners. He said, "I can help you invest and the yields on my plans are very high. In fact, you can invest in my safe bonds and I won't charge you a penny."

After a time the traveler found that his original $25,000 investment in bonds was now worth only $21,000 and it was sinking fast. The supposedly free deal also contained annual expenses and sales charges that were more than he had been earning that year on his bank savings account.

The moral of this lesson is that if you don't spend a few dollars for books and material and take a little time to learn the basics of investing, you can easily end up at the side of the road with your financial wings clipped.

LESSON 26
One More Time
Stay Put in the Market

"History has shown the biggest risk is not being in the market when it drops, but being out of the market when it rises."

This is another lesson about staying in the stock market at all times. I'm going to continue to tell you this lesson until it drives you nuts because it can often mean the difference between a huge and a tiny retirement nest egg. Put these in-structions on your "to do" notes and keep them where you'll see them when the stock market takes an occasional hair-raising dive: History has shown that the biggest risk in in-vesting is not being *in* the market when it drops, but being *out* of the market when it rises. As I look back over my years of investing in the market, I'm glad I avoided trying to time the market. I know it can't be done. Peter Lynch, who set performance records year after year when he was the port-folio manager of Fidelity's Magellan Fund, agrees. He said, "Trying to time the market is a waste of time. I don't know anyone who has been right more than once in a row."

Money and *Newsweek* magazines recently ran feature sto-ries about Anne Scheiber and her astonishing expertise in investing in the stock market. Though she worked as an au-ditor for the IRS, her investment strategy is one that can be used by anyone. She started with a $5,000 investment in blue chip stocks in 1944 and slowly built her nest egg to more than $22 million by the time she died in 1996. She continued to make investments each year through the boom times of the 1950s and 1960s, the recession of the 1970s, and the bull market of the 1980s. Not a risk-taker, Scheiber invested only in well-known companies that made high-quality products. When she died, she owned about 100 different stocks. With careful planning, her average annual return was a whopping 22.1 percent, just a hair under Warren Buffett's 22.7 percent. Had she earned the stock market averages, as measured by the Standard & Poor's 500 stock index, her average annual return would have been only 12.4 percent.

Scheiber was what I call a "standpatter"—someone who buys and holds investments. Her time-tested investment strategy was to buy good dividend-paying blue chip stocks, to avoid worrying about the bouncing stock market, to reinvest the dividends, and to wait for the investments to make her rich.

I've talked with several people over the years who were much like Anne Scheiber. They never earned a lot of money in their jobs but they became wealthy by simply investing regularly and keeping their money working all the time. What struck me about all these people was their ability to overcome hardships, to continue to invest, and to keep their nest egg locked up until they retired.

I asked someone whom I admired, and who had built a fortune from investing small bits of money regularly over the years, what advice he would share from his life that would help other investors.

"In a word: persistence," he said. "Just because everyone else follows the advice of what they see on television, or what they read in the papers or hear from a stock broker, that doesn't mean that you shouldn't trust yourself, or that you shouldn't simply buy and hold stocks and mutual funds. If I had one idea to give people who are striving to build wealth today on a tight budget, it would be let time and persistence work for you."

"That's easy to say," I replied. "But what about when you lose money and the stock market is falling like a rock?"

"Look," he said, "if you want to be successful, you have to go against the conventional wisdom. You have to be willing to stay in the market when everyone is selling. That takes a combination of guts and a belief that, over time, stock prices will always head higher."

"Is that why you don't sell much?" I asked.

He looked at me for a moment. "Yes," he replied. "I don't know anyone who has become rich by selling good stocks. I've found that I make a lot of profit by investing even more money right after a major stock market crash," he said. "The simple old-fashioned principle has always been sound: Buy low and sell high. On the Street it's called "buying on the dips," and over time it has always worked for me. Recently, Wall Street's great bull market has had two big setbacks. The first was in 1987, when I bought at the bottom of the crash. By the mid-1990s, the Dow Industrials had surpassed 5,500, double their high before the 1987 crash. The second major downturn was in July 1996, when the Dow fell to around 5,400 and within a few months bounced back to more than 6,500."

I remember 1987 well. I was on the radio in New York and the media went into a frenzy over Black Monday, when the Dow Jones Industrial Average fell more than 500 points in one day. Back then the Dow was at about 2600 and in one day it plunged 22.6 percent. Investors thought they were slow dancing over the cliff and those who panicked and sold right after the crash thought they saw the big picture, but they were missing a big part of the story—like trying to watch a movie on an airplane without renting the headphones.

What's important to remember is that the two recent stock market corrections (which occurred in 1987 and 1996) are not the same thing as a prolonged bear market (which occurred in the 1970s). A correction is sudden, with panic sweeping Wall Street, and is really just a "blip" in an otherwise strong market. A bear market can last a long time as the stock market continues to slowly decline.

Here's what happened to investors during these two big market corrections. If you had a $10,000 portfolio of stocks just before the 1987 crash, using the market averages of the Standard & Poor's 500 stock index, you had about $8,000 after the crash. If you took out your money in panic and invested it in safe six-month insured certificates of deposits, your money would have grown to about $12,800 by the beginning of 1996. If, however, you just sat on your hands and stayed in the market, you would have reaped a handsome reward, as your money would have grown to about $28,000 by the beginning of 1996. But if you saw the big crash as a signal to invest another $10,000 on the very next day, your money would have grown to $63,500 by the beginning of 1996. After the minicrash in July 1996, I stayed in the market and I bought right after the market hit bottom. Buying when many people wanted to sell, I made 12 percent in just four months.

Mark Hulbert, who writes the *Hulbert Financial Digest,* a newsletter that tracks the performance of financial newsletters, gives this advice: "After you invest, the most important factor in making money in the stock market is discipline. Discipline to stay in the market turns out to play a far more important role than what many investors think," says Hulbert. "Without it, we are like a sailboat without a rudder—buffeted by every change of direction in which the market's wind blows."

I want to say this *again* and say it clearly enough so you'll get the message: If you want to make money in the stock market, *never be out of the stock market.* Find the discipline to hang in there even when a stock market crash has sent many investors to the sidelines.

The lesson we can learn is this: The question isn't what do you think the stock market will do next, the question is what will *you* do next. Based on my experience, if you stay in the market you'll make up your losses and then hang on as the market continues to make new highs.

LESSON 27
But It's Guaranteed
Bond Basis Risk

Now for a scary lesson. Like the weary traveler who kept his purse closed and believed what he was told, you go into a bank and the friendly financial planner tells you, "Don't put your money back into an insured certificate of deposit. I have some government bond funds that are guaranteed and they are safe. You can earn at least 2 percent more interest."

"Sounds great," you say, "and it's guaranteed! Now you've made my day, sign me up."

But what you probably do not realize is that the success of these higher-yielding bond funds the financial planner is touting in such glowing terms is due to the fact that investors who want high yields don't have the slightest idea how much short-term risk they are taking. To make all this work, there has to be a mold somewhere that just keeps churning out these clipped-wing investors. My guess is that the mold is behind the desk in the bank lobby, in front of the phone at the broker's office, or in the ad rooms of the mutual funds.

"Bonds have an unseen danger.
Most people don't know about it, and
therefore it doesn't appear to exist."

A common myth among savers is that bonds earn higher yields but have no more risk than insured certificates of deposit. But it's not true. Nevertheless, millions of people continue to believe that higher yields on long-term bonds come without higher risk, and many of them, when they sell, lose a big chunk of the assets they want to keep safe.

A hysterical woman came up to me at one of my seminars and said, "Look here, Mr. Jorgensen, I put $50,000 into this bond fund and if I want to sell now it's worth only $44,000 and I can't afford to lose any money."

"Why did you invest?" I asked in a soothing tone.

"Because the man told me I could earn higher returns on guaranteed safe government-backed bonds."

"Did you know that this had a risk?" I asked.

"No, and I feel like killing that guy."

I also get a steady stream of letters from people who have worked hard to build up their wealth and want a secure future for themselves and their loved ones. As I write this, I have before me a letter from a reader who wrote, "My sister and I needed to make an interest-bearing investment for our elderly mother who resided in a nursing home. The broker advised me to invest my mother's money in 6 percent Freddie Mac bonds due October 15, 2002. They were safe, he said, and our mother would have a dependable income. Now three years later, our mother has died and my sister wants her one-half of the estate. I called the broker and he told me I could sell the bonds for about $68,000, or $7,000 less than the $75,000 we paid to buy the bonds three years ago. My sister will get her money and I'll have to make up the difference. I feel cheated because I told the broker from the start we wanted safety of principal above all else."

There are a lot of ways to get into trouble when you part with your money, and buying bonds or bond mutual funds is likely to be one of them. They have an *unseen* danger. Most people don't know about it, most salespeople don't talk about it, and therefore it doesn't appear to exist. But it does.

Stay with me a minute and let's go over what a financial planner might say to you. First, you'll be told that all government bonds will be repaid at maturity (as are most corporate bonds), and they are therefore safe. This is correct. What you may not be told, though, is that the guaranteed repayment of the bond at maturity has nothing to do with whether you'll lose money if you sell before maturity and take out your money. That's hard for most people to understand. After all, the offer of much higher interest rates with guaranteed safety is hard to resist.

You can take all the books and friendly advice on bonds and bond funds and roll them into one sentence: The longer your money is out on loan, the more it is at risk. So, in general, the higher the yield of a bond or bond fund, the longer the maturity and the greater the risk.

This danger of investing in bonds is called *bond basis risk.* It's easy to understand if you think about it. Bonds have a fixed rate of return even though interest rates can and do change. If you hold a bond that has five years left to maturity and interest rates rise 1 percent, the market value of your bond could fall about 4 percent, while a 1 percent drop in rates could raise the market price by 4 percent.

Most bond mutual funds, however, want to tout their high yields so they buy long-term bonds that have 25 or 30 years to maturity. Without their knowledge, conservative investors are forced to tread on very thin ice. If interest rates change just 1 percent, the market value of the bonds in these bond funds could rise or fall about 11 percent.

The newspapers carry the price of bonds each day. A typical story might say "The price of the 30-year bond dropped 15/32, to 95-19/32; its yield, which moves in the opposite direction, climbed to 7.11 percent, from 7.07 percent yesterday."

Let me give you the old Wall Street description of bond basis risk: Let's say some time ago you invested $1,000 in a long-term bond paying 7 percent. At the time, it sounded like a good deal, since insured certificates of deposits were paying only 5 percent. Now let's fast-forward to today. The interest rate on a similar new bond is now paying 8 percent. You need some cash, so you call your broker to sell the bond and he says, "It makes no difference if it's a government, corporate, or municipal bond. If you want to sell your old 7 percent bond today, the price is only $920 for your $1,000 bond."

The reason for the plunge in price is obvious. A buyer today can earn 8 percent on a new bond while your old bond pays only 7 percent. You need to sell at a discounted price so that the investor who buys your bond receives a yield as high as the yield on a new 8 percent bond.

The flip side—and there always are winners and losers on Wall Street—is that if interest rates fell to only 6 percent, you might sell your $1,000 7 percent bond for $1,080.

Here I want to say something clearly enough so every reader will hear the message: *Unless you have a money market account, a money market mutual fund, or an insured CD, if interest rates rise, the market value of your bond (or bond mutual fund) will fall.* It makes no difference what anyone tells you, it makes no difference what bond or bond fund you buy, it makes no difference if the bonds are "guaranteed." Take my word for it, if interest rates rise and you sell your bond or bond fund, you can lose money on your investment.

Do yourself a favor. If you are saving long-term for retirement and you don't need the interest income to live on, take the money you have in bonds or bond funds and invest it in the stock market. When you invest in bonds you get about the same sort of price swings as with stocks, yet you miss out on the stock market's inflation-beating returns. In addition, the interest income you earn in bonds is immediately taxable unless you invest in municipal bonds, while gains in stock funds aren't generally taxed until you sell. And these gains may qualify for lower long-term capital gains rates.

Over the long term, as you save for retirement, stocks will at least give you a shot at making decent money and building a much larger retirement nest egg.

LESSON 28
Picking a Winner
Index Funds

Today, financial soothsaying is a great cottage industry. Newspapers, magazines and television continually dance riches in front of our eyes and sometimes we feel like a fool if we don't grab at the latest opportunity to get rich.

Every month, in the personal finance magazines you're enticed by the promise of a hot new mutual fund or stock that's too good to pass up. But the more you learn, the less you should be impressed by fancy magazine stories about top-rated stocks and funds. Because competition is so hot, personal finance magazines often tout stocks that fizzle almost before the ink is even dry on their pages. Keep in mind that stories about where to invest exist primarily to sell magazines.

Or, maybe your broker tells you his brokerage research department is miles ahead of the market in picking just the right stocks for you. Recently, I saw a television commercial for a major stockbroker. The bulls were running up Wall Street in a panic, yet the announcer asserted that with this firm's help, you can not only avoid being trampled by the herd, but know which bull to ride to riches. There's one problem with this ad! The real herd on Wall Street carries briefcases and they panic as often as the cattle.

Almost all of the brokers I've known are honest and professional, but ethics have very little to do with picking stocks successfully. The longer you are in the business you learn that it is very difficult to pick good stocks, and after a flame-out and an unhappy customer you frequently remember the old Wall Street saying: *The market tells the tale.*

If you can't depend on a broker's top picks or on personal finance magazines, consider the plight of the high-profile mutual fund portfolio manager. Other than making appearances on television and being quoted in stories in the magazines to help sell their mutual funds to the public, most of these high-priced portfolio managers are simply not needed to pick the right stocks. It's no secret on Wall Street that most fund managers would look like geniuses if they simply invested in a stock market index, turned out the lights, and went home.

To be honest with you, after 30 years of following the stock market, I've learned that most of what you read and see about investment opportunities is bunk. I'm amazed that people continue to fall for the hype and promises of each new mutual fund. Hey, look at the stars or take a vacation, but don't fall for the fancy promises and open your wallet or purse. Sooner or later you'll lose money and I'm always reminded of the famous question asked at a resort where several stockbrokers had moored their pleasure boats: Where are all the *customers'* yachts?

I can count on the fingers of one hand the number of people who believe that becoming wealthy is simple. Yet, John Bogle, chairman of one of the largest mutual fund companies in America, Vanguard Funds, and someone I respect, believes that investing is not nearly so difficult as it looks. Bogle told me on the air, "If an investor will just buy a general money market fund with the lowest cost for ready cash, a bond index fund and a stock index fund, he owns the three big asset allocation classes that he needs to own and really only needs to think about what portion of each his portfolio should be composed of. A new investor would do well to avoid the hassle of worrying about his or her investments and take the *passive management* route."

Bogle, in a 1996 speech before the Society of American Business Editors and Writers in Chicago, said, "We are developing a form of casino capitalism in the fund industry, in the form of rapid trading in the financial markets and in the mutual fund marketplace." He told the group that his own personal investment principles are: One, he owns funds as long-term investments, and two, he owns passively managed index funds.

Most people who read this book will probably think John Bogle is kidding them. But there's a lot of evidence that he's right. John Bogle's simple investment plan reminds me of a conversation I had with Bob, a guy I met at our church. He's a happy-go-lucky person who doesn't know the first thing about investing his money, so he's kept it safe in the bank. "The stock market," he told me, "is like going over the cliff without a parachute."

"The problem you have," I said, "is that you don't feel comfortable picking a stock mutual fund."

"You're right," he said. "There's just too darn many of them and I don't know where to begin."

"Why don't you just invest in a fund that invests in most of the blue chip stocks and then it's easy to know how you're doing. If the market is up, you're up. If the market is down, you're down."

"That's too easy," Bob said with a smile. "But it's certainly worth a try. What do you call this mutual fund?"

"It's an index fund, and the chances are you'll do better than throwing darts at the 8,000 available funds you can pick from."

What I told Bob was that most *actively managed* stock mutual funds have analysts and portfolio managers who try to pick the best performing stocks and then read their tea leaves as to when to buy or sell them. Mutual funds that use *passive management* let the market earn the results. Without portfolio managers, these funds simply invest in an index and sit on their hands.

They invest in all the stocks that make up the index, which can include stocks of household products, financial companies, drug companies, airlines, and soft drinks. When you invest in such a fund, you should earn the market's average performance, minus the fund's management expenses.

Not very exciting, but history tells us that these passively managed funds (such as the funds that invest in all the stocks that make up the Standard & Poor's 500 stock composite index in the same proportion that each stock makes up the overall index) generally outperform the average managed equity mutual fund. In 1996, according to Lipper Analytical Services, the S&P 500 stock index fund's total return was about 23 percent, and the average stock fund was up 17 percent. Over the past ten years, through December 31, 1996, the average stock fund rose at an average annual 12.5 percent, while the S&P 500 index had risen an average annual 15.3 percent. Lipper also reports that the S&P 500 index has outperformed the average stock fund over the past ten years by a wide margin, returning 314 percent to December 31, 1996, while the average stock fund rose only 260 percent.

The August 1995 issue of *Money* magazine even surprised me. The magazine told its readers about "The new way to make money in funds today. Start with index funds and add the market beaters." *Money* said that few stock funds outperform the market and low-cost, market-tracking index funds do best. The magazine didn't suggest that its readers switch to 100 percent index-tracking funds, but it said index funds should make up the core of one's portfolio.

The June 1996 issue of *Smart Money* magazine gave this advice to its readers: "You can't beat the market—so why even try? The only sensible thing to do is put all your money in an index fund, such as an S&P 500 index fund, and take whatever the market gives you. That's the conventional argument these days, and it's one that has a special resonance considering that 84 percent of all fund managers failed to match the Standard & Poor's 500 stock index last year. Even if you go back ten years, the S&P index has outpaced more than three-quarters of the actively managed competition. A $10,000 investment in an S&P index fund back in 1986 today would be worth more than $40,000."

So why do index funds leave most active portfolio managers and stock-pickers in the dust? They outperform most actively managed funds for four main reasons: They spread the risk of individual stocks by buying a fixed basket of stocks that tend to replicate the entire stock market; they rarely sell (leaving most of the capital gains untaxed until the fund is sold); they stay in the market at all times; and without portfolio managers, they are cheap. How cheap? With some index funds, the fund's annual management charges can be as low as 0.20 percent, compared to as much as 1.75 to 2.00 percent of your assets for a fully managed fund. With so many charges to drag down their performance results, it's no wonder the managed funds start out with a big disadvantage.

Index funds are often scorned by stock-pickers and mutual fund portfolio managers who throw money around at the latest trend, and by those individuals who want a chance to share their latest hot stock with their friends. But I like them because of their simplistic way to invest in the stock market and forget about Wall Street.

Index funds remind me of the old electric typewriters: The best ones are the simple ones. They are quick and easy to use and I don't have to fight the new fancy electronics and gadgets that make life complicated. Maybe it's my small-town background, maybe it's what I learned in years of financial planning, but investments are like old electric typewriters: The best ones are the simple ones. So what do you have to lose? You can go for an old-fashioned simple index fund that, on average, can outperform most of the managed mutual funds, or you can take a chance by throwing darts and see if you hit a winner.

LESSON 29
Spend It or Lose It
IRAs and Retirement Plans at Death

The only sure things in life, the old saying goes, are death and taxes. The Internal Revenue Service may allow you to delay taxes in individual retirement accounts and other retirement plans, but it never forgets that you owe the taxes. Consider this:

- If you take a loss on an investment inside an individual retirement account, you can't deduct the loss against your other income as you could outside these plans.
- When you withdraw your money, every dollar is subject to your ordinary income tax rate. You lose the opportunity to use the possibly lower capital gains tax rate.
- If you need to borrow money, you're out of luck. Assets in an IRA can't even be used as collateral for a loan.
- If you need to use the money in your retirement plan for an emergency, you normally face a hefty 10 percent penalty tax on any money withdrawn before you reach the age of 59½.

Once you retire, however, the IRS expects you to use the money in your retirement plans for living expenses, travel, and sharing your wealth with your heirs. What I know of these IRS rules has shaped my life in particular ways. I no longer think of passing on my retirement plan assets to my kids, because the taxes can wipe out most of my lifetime savings.

George, my neighbor across the street, is retired. A nice fellow who worked hard and made money owning and operating an industrial company that made rubber wheels. Now that he's retired, however, he has a huge pile of money in his individual retirement account and company retirement plans. But George is the type of guy who never spends money unless he can help it. He uses a five-year-old car to take his money to the bank. So I asked him one day what he was going to do with all his money in his retirement plans. "You know," he said, "I just don't need all this money and I'm going to leave it to my kids."

"What worries me, George," I said, "is that I don't think you realize the IRS expects you to spend it now and not leave it to your kids."

George looked at me in wonderment, "They couldn't," he said. "It ain't fair."

"Fair or not," I said, "if you plan to pass on your individual retirement account or company retirement plan assets to someone other than your spouse, you could be in for a big shock. Let's say you have $100,000 in your IRA. These assets will be in your estate at your death and could face federal estate taxes of as much as 55 percent. Let's say you're in only a 40 percent federal estate tax bracket. The value of the asset has now shrunk to $60,000."

By the confused look on George's face, I could tell this was indeed a surprise, and for a guy who liked to hang on to every dollar, this was a real meltdown of his hard-earned money.

"But there's more bad news," I said. "Remember the old rule of 'spend it or lose it'? Well George, that's the IRS's new motto. When your heirs receive your $100,000 retirement plan money, they must pay the income taxes you would have paid had you lived to withdraw the money. If they are in a standard 30 percent federal and state income tax bracket, they lose another $30,000 in taxes.

"So what you're saying is that if I leave my retirement money in my estate and pass it on to my kids, most of my money will go for taxes."

"That's exactly what I'm saying," I said. "But there is one more point you should remember. Federal estate tax forms set off signal flares with the IRS. If you've accumulated more in your individual retirement account than the IRS considers reasonable, you could be hit with an additional 15 percent excess accumulation tax, a penalty tax for doing well. In that case, the $100,000 IRA in your estate you want to leave to your kids might almost disappear without a trace."

Unless you want to face a similar fate when the last spouse to die leaves retirement plans to the kids or heirs, you might consider some options that could reduce your taxes. Giving retirement plan assets to charity can be a big tax saver. The gift lowers the size of your taxable estate, which could save substantial estate taxes. To make a gift to charity, you first have to take the money out of the retirement plan and pay the taxes. Then, when you make the gift, you should get a charitable deduction that will offset the taxes you have to pay on the withdrawal. Gifts and bequests to your kids or other people are normally income-tax free to them, but if you give IRA or retirement plan money, they will have to pay the taxes at their tax rate on money they received from you.

Under current tax law, each person can give up to $10,000 to any individual each year (a couple can give $20,000) without gift taxes. But you can't save up the $10,000 exemptions—each year the opportunity is lost if you don't use it by December 31. Another option is to simply pay the taxes and use the money in your retirement plan for the reason that Congress established the plans in the first place.

If you still intend to pass the IRA assets on to your children, consider carefully your named beneficiary. Making a wrong move, such as failing to name a beneficiary, can affect the size of Uncle Sam's take after your death. That's because who the beneficiary is on your IRA determines what happens to the retirement account. Naming a spouse as a beneficiary is best because bequests to a spouse escape taxes. The spouse can roll over the IRA into a new IRA and choose new beneficiaries. Distributions must then start when the spouse reaches age 70½.

If your other heirs are the beneficiaries, they can always take the money out in one lump sum and pay the income taxes, and because the distributions were "forced" by the account owner's death, they won't pay any 10 percent early withdrawal penalty, regardless of their age. Many new IRA owners, however, want to continue to protect the tax-deferred growth, and then it's important to name a beneficiary.

When someone other than a spouse inherits an IRA, the rules get a bit more complicated. If you inherit an IRA, you can withdraw the account within five years, known as the "five-year rule," and no annual minimum distributions are required.

If your children or other heirs are beneficiaries, the IRA can survive after the owner's death if the original name remains on the IRA account. If the IRA owner dies before 70½, the beneficiaries can spread distributions over their own life expectancy as long as they start withdrawals by the end of the year after they inherit the IRA and keep the account in the owner's name. If the owner dies after age 70½, after the required payouts have begun, then the beneficiaries must take distributions at least as rapidly as the schedule used prior to the owner's death.

If you fail to name a beneficiary, the IRA will revert to your estate and be subject to estate and income taxes, as well as possible probate administration. Then, the account must be liquidated by December 31 of the fifth year after the owner's death. If you have retirement plans in your estate, it pays to seek professional help to determine which is the best way to provide for your heirs.

Is delaying income taxes with an IRA a good idea? That depends on whether you follow the IRS rules and play by their game. An individual retirement account or company retirement plan is a good deal *if* you bite the bullet, pay the taxes, and use the money in retirement.

Now You Have It, Now You Don't
Vesting Retirement Plans

*"Millions of baby boomers and job hoppers
who think they'll retire on big company-
sponsored retirement pay-ins won't."*

Now we're back to another magic act that will haunt millions of American workers in the years to come: Now you have it, now you don't. When you get a new job, chances are that one of the first things the employer will tell you about is its retirement plan and how the company will kick in hefty sums each year into your account. It often sounds like a fast track to riches, but millions of baby boomers and job hoppers who think they'll retire on these big company-sponsored retirement pay-ins won't.

The trouble is that retirement plan rules haven't changed much over the years. In fact, they have remained so set in their ways that they bring to mind the story of Dr. Martin J. Routh, who was president of Magdalen College, Oxford, England, for 63 years, from 1791 to 1854. A lover of old ways, he always clung to his wig and to the fashion of dress of his younger years. Dr. Routh also refused to believe in many of the new inventions that appeared in the 19th century. He steadfastly refused to believe in the existence of trains, and when one of his students arrived from London in only a few hours, he denounced both the student and the trains for conspiring against his sanity.

The Industrial Revolution, however, became such a powerful force that by the late 1800s, it had overtaken the Routhian adherents and begun a chain reaction of inventions and new ideas. One new idea was to offer workers a company-paid pension. But more than 100 years later, most of the people who run company retirement plans still live in Dr. Routh's world and refuse to believe in new ideas.

Pensions in America began with the railroads in the 1880s, when, for the first time, retirement could mean something more than a gold watch; it could mean a monthly income for life. The railroads discovered that they could spread a very low annual cost over 30 or 40 years by offering a pension, and at the same time, when the worker retired, hire younger workers at a much lower salary. It was just good business for the railroads, and what was good business for the railroads in the 1880s was good business for America.

The private pension plans established between 1880 and 1920 were a form of "pension arrangement." They were considered gratuities, not wages, and the business owners were free to pay the benefits or turn them off at will. Workers had no rights in the company-paid plans, and none were ever intended.

The early pension plans established the following rules:

- They provided a defined benefit in advance, based on salary at age 65, usually a fixed lifetime monthly income without any benefits continuing to the widow.

- The retirement benefit was contingent upon working for the same employer for 25 to 30 years, without a break in service, or retiring under the terms of the employer's pension plan.
- The employer was to make all the contributions to the plan.

By the 1980s, the philosophy had changed, and company-paid defined benefit pensions were in retreat for two reasons. First, rising inflation continued to push up salaries on which the retirement benefits were based, and companies were forced to feed a cash-hungry pension system to meet ever-higher monthly retirement checks.

Second, people were living longer and, therefore, collecting more benefits in retirement. The average life expectancy was age 76 years in 1993, according to the U.S. Census Bureau, and is expected to rise to 82.6 years in 2050. On average, that could be almost 70 more inflation-bloated monthly benefit checks per retiree than pension managers estimated just five decades earlier.

Today we have a completely different work environment than when retirement plan rules were established. The average worker no longer works for one company for a lifetime, but changes employers at least six times. And the speed of job hopping has soared in the 1990s. Nearly one in five Americans employed full-time is likely to leave his or her current job in the next year.

With today's downsizing, company buyouts, and restructuring, more and more workers feel that Bruce Springsteen's ballad of the early 1980s now rings true: "They're closing down the textile mill across the railroad tracks. The foreman says these jobs are goin', boys, and they ain't coming back."

The major change today is the shift from employer-paid pensions to employee-employer contribution plans, and the most popular is the 401(k). This plan allows workers to contribute most of the money. It also allows the employer the freedom to decide if the company will make contributions or not, and avoids the high cost of fixed benefit checks to future workers. *Already, more workers are covered by retirement plans that require them to make contributions than are in company-paid pension plans.*

While the concept of employer-sponsored retirement plans has changed, several of the precepts of the original retirement plans of the 1880s have now become part of our American way of retirement. One was the adoption of age 65 as the normal retirement age. This selection was based mostly on the fact that it saved the company a lot of money. In the 1880s, the average life expectancy was only about 47 years and the number of workers who survived beyond age 65 totaled a mere 6 percent of the population. Today, by contrast, the over-age-65 group is growing faster than almost any other in our population. In the past 20 years, the number of Americans age 65 and older has grown by 56 percent to 32 million, and the fastest growing age group is now 85 and older. As a result, pensions and Social Security, which still use a retirement age of 65, are in deep trouble.

Another rule from the original retirement plans was that they were largely a company-controlled arrangement. The benefits were to be paid only to employees who completed the required years of service. If the worker left the company early, the employer didn't want to waste money paying a pension to someone who went to work for another firm. Because the annual pension contributions were paid for by the employer, it was logical, the business owners reasoned, that they should make the rules.

Over the years, the employee's access to the employer's contributions to retirement plans has evolved under the rules of "vesting." With a vesting schedule in its plan, the employer need only allow the worker to "vest" or "earn" the company contributions to a retirement plan in exchange for years of service. This scenario has remained virtually unchanged: If you change jobs over the years, only your vested interest will be there when you leave. To change this rule now and give you full credit for each year you are covered in the retirement plan would increase the cost beyond the reach of many company-sponsored retirement plans.

Why was vesting so important? If the worker left the job without full vesting, some or all of the previous company's contributions made to fund their pension could be used to reduce future company pension pay-ins. Over the years this saved the company a lot of money. For today's worker, however, job hopping and lack of vesting can suck the life out of his or her future retirement benefits like a herd of elephants stomping along a muddy riverbank.

John Butler found me at a seminar, and with his finger pointed at my face, said, "Look here, I spent over four years helping to build this company, then they canned me, and now they tell me all that money they paid into my retirement plan belongs to them."

"Your vesting schedule probably told you that the company's money may never be yours in the first place," I said.

"What do you mean? Who are these guys anyway? I worked my butt off and one of the reasons was that the company was funding a super retirement income."

"Well," I said, "if you had died, become permanently disabled, or the company terminated the plan, you'd get all the company contributions."

"Thanks a lot," he said. "But I just got a pink slip and now I have to start over."

John Butler is not alone. I know what it feels like to have most of my retirement plan assets disappear. It happened when I got a much better job with another company, and since then I've learned everything I could about the vesting schedule in my company retirement plans. I always get a copy of the company's Summary Plan Description Booklet and read it from cover to cover.

Unfortunately, the least-read books in the country are not *The Repair and Maintenance of the Edsel* or *The Rise and Fall of the Byzantine Empire*. Topping both are most company *Summary Plan Descriptions*, or SPD booklets. They are unattractively published, dull, and difficult to read, yet they touch the lives of more than 100 million workers and their families. The SPD is a required part of every private employer retirement plan, and the contents of its action-packed chapters can bring financial catastrophe to millions of Americans each year. If you don't have a copy of your SPD, ask your employer to give you one, and in it, for example, you'll find that if you plan to leave the company, it's important to know the company retirement plan's anniversary date. One more year of coverage in the plan could result in greater vesting and a substantial boost in your retirement plan payout. But if your plan features "instant vesting" and you leave the company before the plan's fifth anniversary date, as John Butler did, you could see all of the highly touted company contributions go up in smoke.

Vesting, in simple English, tells you how much of your employer's previous contributions you can take with you if you leave your job, get laid off, or retire. All of your own contributions from your salary will be returned to you, but the vesting schedule determines how much of the company's money you'll get to keep.

Here's how a typical company retirement plan might work:

- You should become eligible to participate in the plan if you are at least 21 years old and are on the job for at least one year.
- Once you become eligible to join the plan, the company can contribute to your account and you can make tax-deductible contributions yourself through voluntary payroll deductions.
- When you leave the company, your ownership of the company's prior contributions will be based on the vesting schedule in the plan. While vesting schedules can vary among employers, the popular vesting schedules are:

    Gradual vesting. Under this plan, there is no vesting for the first two years, then 20 percent each year thereafter until you are 100 percent vested after a total of seven years in the plan.

Instant vesting. This popular plan does not allow any vesting until you've been in the plan for five years, at which time you become 100 percent vested. Thereafter, all of the company's contributions belong to you.

When you leave your job most employers will say, in effect, "Here's your retirement plan money; come and get it." What you'll be offered is a *lump-sum distribution.* It should include your vested employer contributions, plus your own contributions. It used to be a simple process to transfer this money tax-free to an individual retirement account, but not anymore. The U.S. Labor Department (the agency that oversees company retirement plans) found that only 13 percent of workers given preretirement distributions from their employers actually put the money into other retirement plans or their own IRAs. This was bad news for the government, because the less you have at retirement, the more the government will have to pay out in benefits. So Congress changed the rules. Today, if you want to roll over your lump-sum distribution to your individual retirement account, it's best to give your employer the name and address of your IRA trustee so the check can be sent directly from the employer to your IRA. If you don't have an IRA, open one before you ask for your retirement plan money.

If you take the money and run, you have two options:

1. You can still put the money into your IRA yourself, but in this case the employer will withhold 20 percent of the money as part-payment of future income taxes. If you want to roll over the full amount you'll have to make up the missing 20 percent and

file a request on your federal (and state) income tax
form for a return of the withheld money.

2. If you simply take the cash, however, your money can
    melt before your eyes. First, the employer will
    withhold 20 percent for future taxes. Second, if you
    are under the age of 59½, you'll probably have to pay
    a 10 percent tax penalty. And third, you'll have to
    pay income taxes on every dollar you receive. After
    the smoke clears, you'll be lucky to pocket half the
    money.

The moral of this lesson is that as you change jobs, you
must protect your retirement plan assets or they won't be
there when you retire. This is not play money, it's money
you'll later need for groceries, health care, and clothes. Say
you're 40 years old and you leave your company's retirement plan with a $10,000 lump-sum distribution. You can
take the money and spend it and give away almost half of it
to taxes. Or, you can invest it in a stock mutual fund that
could earn, on average, 15 percent each year and end up
with about $325,000 at age 65. In this case, the choice is
yours: the $10,000 from your company retirement plan
could turn into about $6,000 (after taxes) that you can
spend now, or it could be worth about a third of a million
dollars at retirement.

LESSON 31
Protecting Yourself and Your Family
Disability Insurance

Now let's get serious. The fun and games are over. We're going to talk about real events that can devastate many people's lives at any time. I tell my kids that all the fancy financial planning in the world won't cover the loss of their paychecks. The purpose of this lesson is not to sell you insurance or to suggest that you avoid an insurance salesperson, but to help you understand the basics of disability insurance.

"When you write this book," Bill Thomas told me at a workshop, as he sat in his motorized wheelchair, "be sure to tell the readers what I didn't do. I spent too much money on things I didn't need and almost none on what I really needed—protection from catastrophic loss." He looked at me with deep hurt in his eyes. "I've lost my job, my home, my wife, my self-respect. Tell them that disability is a living hell."

Disability insurance is easy to understand: It provides a monthly income if you have an accident or become ill and can't work. If you acquire no other protection than life insurance, buy a disability policy! From talking to people like Bill Thomas, I believe disability can be a living death. The sudden loss of income is often followed by a psychological depression when extra demands of family members can't be met. The former breadwinner faces the skyrocketing costs of medical care, rehabilitation and recuperation at the same time that his or her ability to earn an income is lost.

Insurance companies say that nearly one in five individuals between the age of 35 and 65 will experience a disability that lasts five years or more, yet only about 18 percent of workers have long-term disability insurance. What's worse, the number of severely disabled people between the ages of 17 and 44 has increased 400 percent in the last 25 years. The reason? Doctors are saving the lives of many patients who would have died a few years ago, but many of them won't be able to go back to work for years, if ever.

Here's the true story of Bob Canty before and after he became disabled. Bob, who was 34 years old, told me he didn't have to worry about becoming disabled because he had a group disability policy at work. I told him to get an individual policy because his group policy was mostly smoke and mirrors. But Bob didn't want to spend the money when he received the coverage free from his employer.

Then I met Bob after he became disabled. He was glued to his wheelchair and he told me a tale of woe. "I didn't know the policy's fine print sucked the life out of the benefits. Look here, Mr. Jorgensen, I was promised $2,000 a month, but I only get about $1,350 a month, and then for only five years, and the coverage is limited to only 24 months for some illnesses."

The wise men in the employer's office, at least the ones I've dealt with, do not come bearing extra gifts; they opt for the half-price sales. You simply sign a card for most company-paid group disability policies and then, if you become disabled, the medical underwriting starts *after* the claim. Group disability policies typically have very restrictive definitions of when you are "totally disabled," so the insurer will look at your medical history, how you became disabled, and if they need to pay the claim at all. The waiting period before benefits are paid can be as long as six months, the policy typically pays only 60 percent of salary (bonuses are usually excluded from coverage) for five years (or in a few cases to age 65 for accidents), and the benefits are usually not portable, so if you leave the company and you have a preexisting health problem, you may find it impossible to buy disability coverage on your own.

If you overcome these obstacles and benefits are allowed, then almost all company group disability plans have an integration level in the contract. Integration (often called "offset") is a fancy word for reducing the disability policy's stated benefits because of other income you may receive while you are disabled. Other income can include benefits received from Social Security, workers' compensation, and some other sources of income. Insurers argue that they are only "protecting" you for the amount in the policy and the other income you may receive can be used to reduce their payouts. And once you are disabled, your benefits are further reduced by the fact that inflation can erode the buying power of the monthly benefit because a cost-of-living feature isn't usually included.

I've spent years in the financial planning business and I can't recall how many times I've talked to people like Bob Canty. In his case, he was promised $2,000 a month in benefits. But his group disability policy, like almost all policies, had a 50 percent "integration level." If he collects $1,000 a month from Social Security and $300 a month from workers' compensation, then his disability benefits can be reduced by $650 a month. In Canty's case, his expected $2,000 a month shriveled to only $1,350.

From a practical point of view, Canty has another problem: His disability benefits will shrink again. If the coverage was paid for by the employer as a company benefit, he'll probably have to scrape up the money to pay income tax on the disability benefits he receives. If he's in only a 15 percent income tax bracket, his net spendable income after taxes falls to about $1,150 a month. This grim news comes to you from someone who has sold company group disability plans.

Why am I telling you this? Some of you are too young to understand that disability can occur at any age, and some of you have forgotten what it would be like to live without a paycheck. The point of this lesson is that you shouldn't skimp on your disability protection. If you are a professional or a wage earner, the smart move is to buy an individual policy that is medically underwritten at the time of application (a medical exam is usually required); normally does not have an integration section in the contract; is *noncancellable* as long as you continue to pay the premiums; and has a *guaranteed annual premium* that can't be increased. The average policy will pay the benefits to age 65 for sickness and for life in the case of accident. Be sure the policy includes a *waiver of premium clause* that will continue to pay the premiums and keep the policy in force after you become disabled. It's also smart to add an inflation factor that will increase benefits each year without requiring a medical exam or proof of insurability. The good news is that, unlike Canty's company group policy, if you pay for the individual policy with your after-tax dollars, the benefits you collect will be income-tax free.

The premium you pay will depend on your age, the monthly benefit you want, and the length of the waiting period (sometimes called the elimination period) before benefits begin. Waiting periods vary from one month to one year, but most individual policies have a 90-day period, which means you'll receive your first check about 120 days after actually becoming disabled. Like auto insurance policies, where the collision damage premium is reduced as the deductible goes up, the longer the waiting period, the lower the premium. A good rule of thumb is that a 90-day waiting period will reduce the premiums by about half as compared to a 30-day period, and a 180-day waiting period will reduce the premiums by about half as compared to a policy with a 90-day waiting period.

What I know of these things has shaped my life. I never needed disability insurance, but I remembered Bill Thomas in a wheelchair and I knew that keeping my individual disability policy in force was the right thing to do.

LESSON 32
Death Protection
Life Insurance

Life insurance is simply death protection. Its purpose is to protect the financial future of your loved ones in the event of your death. How much life insurance you need depends on your personal situation. If you have a home and kids and the loss of your income could be devastating, you need a big chunk. You should plan to cover your mortgage, current debts, college education for the kids and, most important of all, an adequate monthly income for your spouse and family. If you are single, you may need only enough life insurance to wind up your financial affairs, or possibly no life insurance at all.

Before you buy an individual life insurance policy, consider what you want the policy to do. The traditional permanent cash-value policy is a combination of savings and investment. The savings feature allows the insurer to use part of the cash value buildup as a reserve to keep the annual premiums level for life. Cash-value plans have a variety of names, such as whole life, universal life, and variable life. If you want forced savings with tax-deferral on the cash value, and a policy you can't outlive, then you should select a cash-value policy.

The common feature of cash-value policies is that the premiums are as much as four to six times more than those of term insurance, but the policy has the potential to stay in force longer, even to age 100. While these cash-value policies are sold for a lifetime of savings and protection, industry figures show that only 3 percent of the policyholders keep their permanent policies in force for 20 years. "Lapse rates are so high that the turnover is astonishing," an executive of a life insurance company told me. "What's worse," he said, "The consumers who keep their policies have to subsidize those who jump out early."

There are a lot of games kids play in which two things look alike, but only one is the correct answer. My kids drove me nuts with these games because they already knew the answers.

"Look, dad," my daughter said, "How can you be so dumb?"

"I don't know," I said. "Each answer looks good to me."

What you're going to read next is like the kid's game with only one correct answer. The hefty cash values and the death benefit look like they are both part of a cash-value policy, but the cash values have a way of disappearing while the death benefit remains. That's because when you die, the typical policy requires the use of your cash value to help the insurance company pay part of the death benefit. If you also have a policy loan outstanding, the insurer will decrease the amount it pays your beneficiaries by the amount of the loan. Let's say you have an old cash-value life policy with a death benefit of $100,000. But if your cash-value savings amount to $40,000 you really only have $60,000 of pure death protection (the death benefit less the cash value.) The bottom line is this: As long as you keep the whole-life policy in force, the cash value belongs to the insurer, not to you. And if you cancel the policy, you'll pay income taxes on the earnings inside the contract—just as you would with an individual retirement account. At your death, however, the death proceeds of any life insurance policy are received by the beneficiaries income-tax free.

Another alternative is a term policy. Term life insurance is like auto insurance; you pay a premium for a year's coverage and it covers only that year's protection. You are, in effect, renting the death protection. Typically, the cost of term insurance increases each year as you get older, but if your objective is maximum death protection at the lowest cost for a specific time frame, even as long as 20 years, then you should investigate term life insurance. This is the type of life insurance folks typically use to cover the period when the mortgage is the highest or they have to save to educate their children.

Term policies come in two basic types: increasing annual premiums called annual renewable term (ART), and level-premium term. If your concern is locking in premiums and benefit guarantees for 5, 10, 15, or 20 years, then you'd want level-premium term. However, if your need for life insurance will expire in five years or less, then look at the increasing premium type.

A third type of policy is a decreasing term policy in which the annual premiums remain the same but the death benefit declines each year. These policies are most often purchased as a way to pay off a mortgage on the theory that, while the death benefit declines each year, so does the mortgage loan balance.

The last type of life insurance is guaranteed-issue. This is the stuff that finds its way into your mailbox or your Sunday newspapers. This expensive life insurance is offered without a medical exam or other health questions. The typical policy is issued between the ages of 55 and 80 with a maximum death benefit of $25,000. However, because the policy is issued without medical information, if death occurs from illness within three years of policy issue for ages 55 to 64, or two years for ages 65 to 80, typically the company will return only the premiums paid plus 5 percent interest. If death occurs from an accident at any age, the company will typically pay the full death benefit in the policy, plus the premiums paid plus 5 percent interest.

Because the odds of dying are the same no matter what kind of policy you buy, I have found that most people look at price. A typical $200,000 cash-value policy with a saving plan for a nonsmoking male age 35 might cost $1,005 a year at today's interest rates. But this savings plan won't do much good if what you really need is life insurance protection. In that case, a 15-year level-premium term policy for the same nonsmoking individual might cost only $162 a year. But there is no free lunch at the term life insurance counter. When your level-term policy expires at age 50, and if you are in good health, the annual premiums for another 15-year level-term $200,000 policy can increase threefold to about $552 a year. Then at age 65, if you are still healthy and remain a nonsmoker, another 15-year level-term policy could cost $2,460 a year.

When you apply for life insurance, there are four basic premium levels:

1.   The cheapest premium is reserved for *Super Preferred Nonsmokers* (SPNS). This is the low rate you see in many advertisements, but to fall into this class you have to resemble the guy in the old Charles Atlas ads on the beach, kicking sand into people's faces. And, in many cases you do. To qualify for the SPNS rates you must not have smoked cigarettes, pipes, or cigars or used any form of smokeless tobacco within the past 12 months or longer. You must be in excellent health, have a low cholesterol/HDL ratio, no history of alcohol or drug abuse, blood pressure less than 140/90, and no parent or sibling with coronary artery disease or cerebrovascular disease prior to

the age of 60. You must also have a clean driving record and not engage in hazardous activities, such as skydiving, flying airplanes, bungee jumping, or motor sports.

You won't need a magnifying glass to find out if you qualify for the best rate, but you may have to change out of your superman costume to take the medical exam. If you do qualify for the new SPNS rates, life insurance can be purchased for a very low premium. You may still qualify for the preferred nonsmoker (PNS) rate at a somewhat higher premium if you have one or more items that disqualify you for the lowest rate.

2. The next level of premiums are for *Nonsmokers* (NS). This rate is for individuals who don't smoke, are in good health, but don't qualify for the SPNS or PNS rate.

3. The next level is reserved for *Smokers* (SK). The smoker rate is for individuals who smoke tobacco, are in good health, and otherwise qualify for the policy.

4. The next level is *Rated* policies. Extra premiums can apply to individuals who have a history of medical problems. The most common conditions that result in "rated" policies are diabetes, substance abuse, hazardous avocation, obesity, hypertension, coronary artery disease, and cancer. Depending on the health risk, insurers can rate the premium from A to G, or 1 to 16. The higher the rating, the more the standard premium is increased. The good news is that most people with a health problem can buy life insurance.

The annual premiums may be one, two, or more times above the standard rate, but coverage is typically available for someone who needs protection.

What has amazed me is how the cost of life insurance has declined over the years. As a result, you simply can't skimp on your life insurance protection. Here are some sample annual premiums for a $100,000 ten-year level-premium term policy:

Age	SPNS	NS	SK
35, male	$151	$202	$ 365
35, female	134	175	300
55, male	518	760	1,460
55, female	348	501	970

SPNS = Super Preferred Nonsmoker, NS = Standard Nonsmoker, SK = Smoker

Buying life insurance has also changed over the years. When I was an agent, you only purchased life insurance from a life insurance agent and you were either in good health or you were rated (called substandard) and paid a higher premium. Today, you can buy individual life insurance from an agent, a bank, a broker, a financial planner, by phone, and on the Internet, and your personal habits count as much as your health.

If you plan to buy life insurance from an agent, be sure to select one who represents more than one insurer with top financial ratings, and look for someone who is a Chartered Life Underwriter (CLU) or a Chartered Financial Consultant (ChFC). From my years in the insurance business, I know how hard it was to become a CLU, and while these designations do not guarantee the best agent, they at least suggest that the person was serious enough to take the ten college-level courses needed to earn the degree.

The latest innovation is to bypass the agent and sell life insurance directly to individuals by telephone and the mailbox. Companies that specialize in finding the cheapest term life insurance began to appear in the late 1980s. Today, ads for shopping services can be found all around you, especially on the radio, in newspapers, and in magazines. The shopping services have three common features. First, one brief call may find you the best bargains in term insurance. That's because term insurance lends itself to computerized comparisons. Second, an agent does not visit you. All activity is over the phone, fax, and by mail. Finally, all shopping services are licensed insurance agencies. Their compensation comes from the insurance company after you have accepted the insurance by paying the premiums due.

But at this point the similarity ends. Some buying services represent only one company, but will illustrate a variety of plans from that one company. Others have only a few companies and may not add new companies often. A few companies are truly independent. If they update an extensive database monthly, and quote only financially strong insurers, you've probably found the right combination.

I wondered about these shopping services, so I called one from a big newspaper ad. Without asking extensive questions about my health (or that of my family) or my lifestyle, I was told, "Boy, do we have a good deal for you. The premium is so low you won't believe it." It turned out I couldn't believe it. They were selling a lemon with a rolled-back odometer in a bait-and-switch approach. Once they had my application, the premiums they quoted took off like a rocket.

A second caveat is that some buying services offer plans with a mix of guaranteed and variable rates. For example, in a 20-year level-premium term plan, rates may be guaranteed for only the first five years and estimated thereafter. Many insurers will, however, guarantee rates and annual premiums for a full 20 years at comparable premiums. But, again, there is no free lunch at the insurance counter. The longer the premium rate is guaranteed, the higher the first annual premium. For example: $250,000 term life for a male non-smoker age 45 has a first-year annual premium of $235 for annual renewable term (ART), but a $463 premium when the rates are guaranteed for 15 years.

$250,000 term life age 45 male preferred nonsmoker

Year	Age	Annual premium	10-yr. level premium	15-yr. level premium
1	45	$ 235	$ 395	$ 463
5	49	680	395	463
Total 5 yrs.		2,218	1,975	2,315
6	50	883	395	463
10	54	1,530	395	463
Total 10 yrs.		8,210	3,950	4,630
Total 15 yrs.		12,745	8,063	6,945

Any life insurance agent who is pounding the street look-ing for prospects will tell you that a lot of business comes from selling life insurance to pay estate taxes. In my own case, years ago, I also spent most of my time looking for peo-ple with hefty estate tax problems. Today, the industry has come up with a new policy to help pay estate taxes, a *Second-to-Die* (Survivorship) policy that jointly covers two lives and pays the benefit only at the death of the last insured, usually a spouse. This policy is generally much cheaper than two single-life policies, and because all assets left to a spouse at the first death are estate-tax free, the policy is designed to pay the estate taxes at the death of the surviving spouse.

If you remember Murphy's Law, you'll remember that nothing seems to go right. Well, Murphy must be selling a lot of life insurance! He was around when I was in the business years ago, and he's still at his trade today because most of the life insurance sold to pay estate taxes is sold in a way that actually *increases* estate taxes, instead of reducing them. Most agents won't tell you this because they fear it will make it more difficult to sell you life insurance. I know this sounds crazy, but it's true. Say you buy a $500,000 life insurance policy to help pay your estate taxes and you are the owner of the policy and pay the premiums. At your death, the $500,000 can come right back into your estate, and with a possible 55 percent estate tax level, $275,000 of this money could go right back to Uncle Sam in taxes. You are paying premiums for half the benefits, and the government gets the other half!

To avoid this mess and get every dollar you paid for, you should not be the *owner* of the policy. Why am I telling you this? Because, if you don't own the policy, it's not your property and it won't be includable in your estate for estate tax purposes. As a result, your heirs will get the full tax-free $500,000. Rather than owning the policy yourself, the policy could be owned by an irrevocable life insurance trust, which is outside your estate. Or, your kids (or other heirs) could own the policy and pay the premiums from the annual gifts you make to them. Each person can give up to $10,000, or a couple jointly $20,000, tax-free gift to any individual each year. The recipient pays no income tax on these gifts. If you are interested in using life insurance to pay your estate taxes, it pays to seek professional help before you buy the policy.

If you already have an old life insurance policy, here are some ways to cut your cost:

- Pay your premiums annually. Installment payments can cost you from 6 percent to as much as 10 percent of the premium to cover the insurer's billing costs.
- Reduce your policy's face amount if your circumstances change and you need less insurance. If you have a cash-value policy, a lower death benefit will reduce future payments and save the cash for later on. Once you've reduced the death benefit, however, you can't later go back and increase it without new medical information and possibly a new application.
- Apply for cheaper "nonsmoker" rates if you've quit smoking for at least a year and your old policy was issued as a "smoker." Your annual premiums could be cut in half.

When you apply for insurance, do you ever wonder how the insurance companies learn about your risk of dying from a heart attack, how often you skydive, your driving habits, and other personal information? It's easy. It takes about two minutes to plug into the insurance industry's huge database at the Medical Information Bureau (MIB) near Boston.

All insurers use this database to help them underwrite your applications for health, life, or disability policies. The MIB records are updated every time you apply for insurance. Because the watchdog group at the MIB is looking over your shoulder, it's a good idea to be completely honest about your medical and personal history when you apply for insurance.

To learn more about the MIB, write for its free booklet, *The Consumer's MIB Fact Sheet,* and for instructions on how to request a copy of your personal file. Write to: MIB, Box 105, Essex Station, Boston, MA 02112.

In this "I want it now" era of handy credit cards and bank loans, life insurance is one of the most unusual purchases most individuals will ever make. It requires us to sacrifice our current lifestyle and pay for a future event that might not happen while the policy is in force. But the payoff is a worry-free future for yourself and your loved ones and the knowledge that you have your priorities on track.

LESSON 33
The Last Resort
Social Security

I love getting things done right away. That way, I don't have to remember to finish a task and I know it's done. Our son, however, drove us crazy when he waited until the last minute to study for an exam when he was in school. And, as I've traveled through life, I've found that many people are like my son: They delay to the last minute the important things like saving for retirement.

Today, Social Security covers about 141 million workers, but it pays benefits to 43 million people, almost one-third the number paying into the system. More than nine out of ten Americans who are age 65 or older receive Social Security benefits. And here's the bad news for those who waited until their later years to start saving for retirement: The Social Security Administration says that 13 percent of all retirees have no other income but their monthly benefit check and live in poverty. Another 24 percent rely on Social Security for 90 percent of their total income. Even with this grim news, many baby boomers and twentysomethings will fail to put aside some money each month and Social Security will also become their last resort in retirement. Now we're getting close to the bottom line on anyone's retirement future.

"A worker born in 1960 or later will have to wait to age 67 to collect full Social Security benefits."

The *unseen* danger most people overlook is that even though they'll pay sharply higher Social Security payroll taxes over their lifetime, they'll be lucky if Social Security provides for more than a quarter of what their preretirement income was.

Unless you've been living under a rock someplace, you probably already know this. You should also know that Congress will continue to change the way Social Security pays benefits, and anyone under age 50 today will find that they have to work longer on the job and collect less at retirement. Without these changes, future retirees will have to depend on the willingness (and ability) of younger workers to pay thousands more in taxes, or the government will have to borrow trillions of dollars, or Social Security benefits may be slashed by a third or more.

How did we get into this mess? It's simple. The original Social Security bill established a trust account for each beneficiary that would later pay that person's benefits. But, over the years, Congress has spent the money that was to be held in trust to pay each worker's future retirement benefits. The result: Social Security is now a pay-as-you-go system in which today's workers pay for the retirement benefits of today's retirees.

When President Roosevelt announced the birth of Social Security in 1935, everyone who worked on the bill knew that in time, the rising benefits paid to a growing number of older beneficiaries would become incredibly expensive. As recounted in the Morgenthau diaries, Harry Hopkins, head of the Federal Emergency Relief Administration, who had just seen the startling figures projecting billions of dollars of spending, put in a phone call to another member of the committee, Treasury Secretary Henry Morgenthau, Jr. The phone conversation about the future payouts went like this:

Morgenthau: Not this year, but it's the thing that it runs into.

Hopkins: Well, there are going to be twice as many old people 30 years from now, Henry, than there are now.

Morgenthau:	Well, I've gotten a very good analysis of this thing and I'm going to lay it on her lap [Frances Perkins, Secretary of Labor] this afternoon. I'm simply going to point out the danger spots, and it's up to someone else to say whether they want to do it. I'm not trying to say what they should do—I want to show them the bad curves.
Hopkins:	That old age thing is a bad curve!

The bad curve they were talking about is the declining ratio between those who pay into the system and those who receive benefits. In 1947, 22 active workers supported each person receiving benefits; today it's more like three active workers for each beneficiary. And, in about 12 years, the baby boom generation will begin to retire and they will cease paying Social Security taxes, live longer than previous generations (the average life span has increased a whopping 14 years just since Social Security was created), and start drawing out benefit checks. So, in the future, Social Security will have fewer workers paying in and more retirees living longer beyond age 65 and collecting a lot more benefit checks. And if that weren't enough to frighten anyone but the eternal optimist, living standards will rise faster than they did a generation ago and the benefit checks will continue to increase.

My daughter, who has her father's trait of saving a buck, said to me, "You know dad, I know that Social Security is in deep trouble when more kids my age (under 35) believe in UFOs than think they'll ever receive a check from Social Security."

Unlike my daughter, and people who believe in UFOs, I have no doubt that the Social Security program will continue into the future. The problem is that while most people are now aware that Social Security will probably pay less in the future, they don't realize that they will have to make up the difference between what they expected to collect and what they will actually collect when they retire.

Most people also mistakenly believe that if they paid their Social Security taxes over the years, then their benefits are not a gift from the government, but rather a guaranteed return on their payments into the system. But Social Security never made any guarantees to the American worker. A wall poster, posted on employees' bulletin boards when Social Security taxes were first taken out of paychecks, clearly states that *there is no guarantee that the funds collected will ever be returned to you.*

The point of this lesson is not that retirement can't have a happy ending. The point is that you have to start now to make it happen. You also have to start saving now to replace the money you might have expected from Social Security. With a tidal wave of aging baby boomers approaching retirement age, here's what you're likely to find from Social Security in the coming years:

You'll collect benefits later in life. If you were born before 1937, your "normal" retirement age continues to be age 65, with benefits reduced to 80 percent of those at age 65 if you retire at age 62. But if you were born after 1937, your "normal" retirement age is going up gradually. For example, a worker born in 1943 won't receive the full benefits until age 66, and those born in 1960 or later will have to wait

NOTICE

Deductions from Pay Start Jan. 1

Beginning January 1, 1937, your employer will be compelled by law to deduct a certain amount from your wages every payday. This is in compliance with the terms of the Social Security Act, sponsored and signed by President Roosevelt, August 14, 1935.

The deduction begins with 1%, and increases until it reaches 3%.

There is no guarantee that the fund thus collected will ever be returned to you. What happens to the money is up to each congress. No benefits of any kind before 1942.

This is NOT a voluntary plan. Your employer MUST make this deduction. Regulations are published by the Social Security Board, Washington, D. C.

until age 67. And early retirement benefits will also gradually diminish. For someone who must wait to age 67 to collect full benefits, the benefits at age 62 will be reduced to only 70 percent of those at age 67. For people in their 20s, the future is grim. Congress is already talking about raising the "normal" retirement age to 70.

Why the higher retirement age? People are living longer, goes the argument, so most people can continue to work well past age 65. But the real reason for the higher retirement age is that Social Security does not pay benefits to someone in the cemetery. With the higher retirement ages, a lot of people will not live long enough to collect full retirement benefits and the system will save a bundle of money.

You'll pay more in taxes. Each year the amount of your earned income subject to Social Security payroll taxes increases (in 1997, it's $65,400, up from $62,700 in 1996), and Congress is sure to also hike the current payroll tax rate of 6.2 percent for both the worker and the employer.

You'll get lower monthly benefits. This is done very quietly by lowering the "replacement rate," or the amount of Social Security benefits compared to the worker's preretirement income. Currently, for a retiree at age 65 whose annual salary has been $40,000, the replacement rate is 33 percent; with a $50,000 annual income, the rate drops to only 28 percent. In the future, for many retirees, the replacement rate could drop to as low as 20 percent.

You'll be taxed more. If you have a good income in retirement, you can expect to pay more in Social Security taxes. Forget about the fact that you paid the same rate of payroll taxes as everyone else. Currently, if your income (all income including income from pensions, municipal tax-free bonds, and half your Social Security benefits) in retirement is less than $32,000 for married couples, and $25,000 for singles, you'll pay no taxes on your benefits. But if your income is between $32,000 and $44,000 married, or between $25,000 and $34,000 single, you can pay income taxes on 50 percent of your benefits. If you earn more than these limits, you can pay taxes on 85 percent of your Social Security benefits.

Keith Henderson, who I know has done very well financially over the years with his investments and real estate, told me that now that he faces retirement, he'll have to pay a penalty for his success.

"Look here, Jim," he said, "I took the government's advice and I made and saved a lot of money, but now that I'm retired, they want to tax my benefits as much as 85 percent. What I don't understand is that I didn't pay taxes when I put money into my company retirement plans and I pay taxes when I take the money out. That's fine. But with Social Security, I paid income taxes on the contributions and they now want to tax me all over again on the money I take out. Is that fair?"

"Good question," I said, "but it has absolutely nothing to do with fairness. The bottom line is that Congress has found that people like you who made and saved money over the years can afford to pay the taxes. It's a good source of revenue for the government."

"All right, but from what I hear, Congress is working on a means test that would deny full benefits to those with high incomes in retirement. If that goes into effect, what the hell good is Social Security?"

"You have a good point," I said, "but understand this: Social Security is really a transfer tax from the rich to the poor. The more you have in retirement, the less you'll get from the system."

"Well there's one good point in all of this," he said.

"What's that?" I asked in wonderment.

"At least they can't tax me on 85 percent of my benefits if they don't pay them to me in the first place, can they?"

"Keith," I said, "don't be too sure, they're probably working on that."

What Congress *is* working on is a means test. For example, one idea floating around Congress is that retirees with annual incomes of more than $35,000 a year could have their benefits reduced on a sliding scale starting at 7.5 percent and going up an additional 5 percent for every $10,000 of extra annual income.

Your benefits can be reduced. If you retire, collect Social Security, and continue to work in retirement, your benefits can be reduced. According to *USA Today,* some 70 percent of baby boomers (people born between 1946 and 1964) now expect to continue to work after they "retire." Many won't be able to afford to retire as their parents did, others will be "downsized," and others will have started their own business. Social Security loves this trend because it won't have to pay full benefits to most people who continue to work and it will continue to collect payroll taxes from the postretiree workers.

Bill Jackson is not rich like Keith Henderson. He's a guy who just got by raising a family and living from paycheck to paycheck. "Look here," he told me at a workshop, "I didn't save enough during my working years and my Social Security benefits aren't enough to live on so I have to continue to work. But if I continue to work, I lose a big chunk of the benefits I've already paid for just when I need them the most. What the hell is going on? I paid my taxes and now the government says I can't collect. Worse yet," Bill screamed at me, "because I have to continue to work, I have to pay Social Security taxes on my wages for benefits they won't give me!"

By the confused look on his face, I knew he was looking for an answer. But I didn't have one. Bill's problem goes back to the inception of Social Security right after the Great Depression, when the Act was intended to compel people to retire and thus create more jobs for younger workers. One way to accomplish this was with an "earnings test" so that any earned income on the job above the annual limits would reduce or eliminate Social Security benefits. For those who continue to work, in spite of the earnings test, the IRS and Social Security will clip their income and benefits like twin buzz saws. Seniors will pay federal and state income taxes and Social Security taxes on their earnings, and then face the loss of most or all of their Social Security benefits. This means that many working seniors will find that they're taking home much less than half of what they are earning on the job.

Today Bill Jackson is not alone. More and more retirees now feel they have to continue to work to make ends meet. Hearing the howls of anger from the folks back home,

Congress has increased the earnings limit (income earned on the job) for people age 65 to age 69 to $13,500 for 1997, to $14,500 in 1998, and to $30,000 by 2002. Over these limits, retirees lose $1 of benefits for every $3 of earnings. After age 70, there is no earnings test. But retirees below age 65 are hit two ways: the earnings test is still stuck at a low $8,640 a year for 1997 and they lose $1 of benefits for every $2 of earnings over that limit.

Well, what can you do? Unless you want to be stuck in the no-win situation of continuing to work and paying taxes while you lose your Social Security benefits, you should start now to save enough money to make up the difference in what you'll actually collect from Social Security in the future and what you'll need in retirement. Social Security lists maximum monthly benefits based on your earnings. As of July, 1995, for retirees aged 65 and a preretirement annual income of $10,800, the maximum benefit for the worker was $520 a month, with a spouse, $708. With average preretirement earnings of $23,900, the maximum monthly benefit was $860, with spouse, $1,290, and for high earners whose incomes were $60,600 or more, the maximum monthly benefit for the worker was $1,200, with spouse, $1,800.

Social Security has made it easy to check up on your payroll tax records and get an estimate of your benefits in retirement by filling out a *Request for Earnings and Benefit Statement.* You can get the form SSA-7004 by calling Social Security at 800-772-1213, or stopping by your local Social Security office.

LESSON 34
Someone to Help You
Financial Planners

If you are unsure how to invest your money, you may be thinking about turning to a financial planner for help. But the financial planning industry has changed dramatically over the past few years, so first you need to determine what help you need.

If you have less than $25,000 to $50,000 to invest, chances are that your business won't be worth the traditional financial planner's time. If you do seek a traditional financial planner, do your homework first. The worst mistake you can make is to turn over your money to a financial planner without first understanding how the money is to be invested and what it will cost you to use his or her services. After all, you wouldn't let a stranger drive your car. Why should you let one handle your money? For that matter, why should you let one invest your money with every idea that comes your way?

Gary Wollin of Wedbush Morgan Securities in San Francisco, a broker with 30 years on Wall Street, offers these four rules for losing money in the stock market in the shortest amount of time:

1. Buy whatever the telephone call is about. You'll probably talk to a broker who will fill your ear with his or her past conquests. You'll get calls for oil and gas wells, coins, Scotch, wine, and every other hot idea under the sun. These people will help you invest your money until it's all gone. If you give your money

to a stranger on the telephone, your chances of losing it are very great. Or, as Al Capone once said, "Anyone found sleeping in the trunk of a car deserves to be shot."

2. Never, but never take a loss. This rule, at first, may seem like nonsense. How can I lose a great deal of money if I never take a loss? It's simple. Buy a stock at $40 and hold on to it as it declines. Now it's selling at $12. "Well," you say, "if I haven't sold it, I really haven't lost anything." The problem is that the stock probably won't get back to what you paid for it. One of the secrets of investing is to know when to cut your losses. If you expect to always make a profit in the stock market, you're in for disappointment.

3. Follow the stock tips. Brokers and financial planners are in the business to give you stock tips. So are your friends. Often a person buys 1,000 shares of a $50 stock because some stranger he or she met on a golf course told him or her that the stock was sure to go up. The basic fact is that no one knows for sure when a stock will go up. Often, by the time you buy the "hot" stock, it's already on its way down in price.

4. Try to become rich fast. Lack of patience is probably the biggest single impediment to success in the stock market. With Wall Street and the media focusing on the big winners, most investors get the unrealistic expectation that they can win right away, and win big every time. Investing in the stock market is a long-term (over five years) project. The correct approach is to have the patience to get rich slowly. (Reprinted by permission of Gary A. Wollen.)

Before you begin your search for a financial planner, there are certain facts you need to know.

How financial planners are paid.

- *Commission-only.* This old-time method of one-on-one personal service is almost extinct. The services of such planners are free; they make their money from the sales commissions on annuities, mutual funds, and other products that you buy.
- *Fee-based.* These planners will charge you a fee for developing a financial plan and typically earn commissions on any product they later sell you. Once you've paid the planner's fee, you have no obligation to invest, but many planners will reduce their planning fee if you do.
- *Fee-only.* These planners work much like an accountant or lawyer, charging only for their time on an hourly basis. They do not sell any financial products. The initial fee can run between $500 to $5,000, depending on the planner, your assets, and your age. Before you use a fee-only planner, be sure to set limits on the cost and the work to be done. Many fee-only planners also provide a program to monitor your investments, usually for a charge of 0.5 percent to 1.0 percent per year on the assets you have under management.
- *Annual-fee.* This is the fastest-growing segment of the financial planning business. Here you may pay a fee (usually from $100 to $500) for a one-shot personal financial report. In all cases, the planner, investment adviser, or account representative helps you purchase no-load or low-load funds. The adviser also provides quarterly statements of your account. You can find

annual-fee planners in your town, or nationwide in what has become known as the "no-load fund bazaar" investors' services. National firms like Charles Schwab, Smith Barney, American Express Advisors, and Merrill Lynch all offer annual-fee programs.

Typically, the fee of annual-fee services is between 1.25 percent to 1.50 percent of the assets under management each year. Most funds you buy will also have a 12-b(1) fee of 0.25 percent per year to help pay for advertising and payments to the adviser. But this hand-holding isn't cheap. These annual fees are *in addition to* the regular annual management fees of the mutual funds.

How to look for a professional planner. Finding a good financial planner today is a lot like trying to roller-skate in a room filled with marbles. Not only must you navigate a maze of investment products and often indecipherable industry jargon, but you must also be sure the investments you do make will let you sleep at night.

Many people who purport to be financial planners report their activities to almost no one. Some financial planners are little more than single-product salespeople with little or no government or trade supervision. Others are professionals who face industry and federal regulators. And, some planners have little formal education, while others have a bachelor's or master's degree with professional designations.

The initials after a planner's name do not guarantee competence nor ethics, but they do indicate that the planner has made an effort to become a professional by completing a two-year college-level course and passing as many as ten separate examinations.

The most popular professional designations are Certified Financial Planner (CFP), Chartered Financial Consultant (ChFC), and Chartered Life Underwriter (CLU). If I were to meet with a planner, I'd want to see one or more of these degrees hanging on the wall. I'd also want the planner to be a Registered Investment Advisor under the Investment Act of 1940 and registered with the Securities Exchange Commission (SEC).

If the planner is registered with the SEC, the most important document is the "Disclosure Statement," which must be given to prospective clients before any work begins. This document outlines the services, fees, education and background, and any other business the planner does. You should receive a copy of this at your first interview; sign it and keep it for your files.

After you've selected several financial planners for consideration, make an appointment to visit them in their offices. The initial visit is normally without charge. Here is where you learn what the planner can do for you and whether or not you feel comfortable with the person and the process. I suggest you pose a problem on how to invest some of your money. If the answer is in line with your comfort zone, you know you have a planner who thinks like you do. If the answer fills you with scary visions of financial ruin, you know you're in the wrong office.

Several organizations and associations will provide you with the names of financial planners in your area if you call them.

Here are the best sources:

- The International Association of Financial Planners (IAFP) will send you the names of its five best-qualified planners with professional designations in your area. Call the IAFP at 800-945-IAFP.
- The American Society of CLU and ChFC will send you the names of up to five planners in your area and a booklet, *How to Pick a Good Professional Planner.* Call them at 800-243-2258.
- The National Association of Personal Financial Advisors (NAPFA) will send you a list of fee-only planners in your area, a booklet, *Why You Should Select a Fee-Only Planner,* and an interview sheet with questions to ask on your first interview. Call them at 888-FEE-ONLY.
- The Institute of Certified Financial Planners will send names and biographies of three of its planner members in your area, along with a brochure, *How to Select a Qualified Financial Planner,* which includes 12 key questions to ask a planner. Call them at 800-282-7526.

LESSON 35
Make Every Penny Count
Tips on Saving Money

My father told me, and I told my kids, to run a household like a business. Maybe your household income is not as large as that of IBM or Ford Motor Company, but it's all you've got and it's important to make every penny count. What I'm talking about is the pit in your stomach that tells you each day that you're living from paycheck to paycheck, that your personal finances resemble a bowl of spaghetti in midexplosion, and a sizable retirement nest egg continues to remain beyond your grasp.

Here are some of the rules and habits I've followed and passed on to my kids for financial success:

Establish a budget. Most American high schools teach driver training, but almost none teaches family finances. In case you didn't learn basic financial planning in school, the number one requirement to start building wealth is to make a budget. But the word "budget" doesn't mean skimping, passing up the good times, or depriving yourself of a night out. With a budget, you'll get more—not less—out of the money you spend.

"The purpose of a budget is to force you to spend less than you make."

The secret of making a budget work is to pay yourself first, then allocate the balance of your income to those bills you must pay each month. Now you know how much money is left over and what you can spend on everything else. The important thing to understand is that it's okay to pay yourself first. You don't have to feel guilty about socking away some cash for emergencies and long-term savings. Chances are, you'll find money you never realized you had.

If you only pay the bills you receive, follow the farmer's advice and make up a bunch of bills from YOU, INC. and give them to a friend. Then each month in the mail you'll get the bill for "savings." Start out saving 5 percent of your monthly take-home pay, and after you've paid all your bills, live on the balance. Later on, after you develop the skills of budgeting, you can increase the amount you save to 10 percent. And, if all else fails, use a cookie jar and take $3 out of your wallet or purse and put it in the jar each day. That's $1,086 a year, and in five years, invested in stock funds, you could have over $7,500. In ten years, this cookie jar method of saving and investing could amount to about $25,000. Not a lot of money, but at least you'll learn that even small change can later on change your life.

Once you've developed a monthly budget, put it in a visible place (like the front of the refrigerator) where you can continually check up on your progress. A budget put away in a drawer is a dead budget. Try to stay within your budget and make the necessary adjustments when conditions change. Put down in writing everything you spend. This should enable you to gain control over your personal finances. I can promise you that if you are dedicated to staying within your budget, your life and personal finances will change for the better.

Cut your plastic payments. If you don't need all the money you have in savings, first use as much of this money as you can to pay off your credit card debt. Allocate your money each month so you can pay off the credit card with the highest interest rate first. Then, when you've paid that card off, go to the next one. Make getting out of debt your jumper cables to a better life.

You don't have to be a math teacher to know that you'll never get rich earning 5 percent on $100 of savings at the bank while you pay someone else 18 percent interest on $100 of credit card debt. Simple math should tell you that if you earn $5 of income and lose $18 in interest, you're going in the hole $13 for every $100. And your rickety house of financial cards can be hit again: the IRS won't let you take a tax deduction for the credit card interest and it will sock you income taxes on the interest you earn at the bank. The grim news is that after tax, your 5 percent interest income may be only about $4, and after you've paid taxes on your income, your losses on $18 of credit card interest can cost you about $22. It's enough to make a grown person reach for a box of Kleenex.

If you carry a monthly balance on your credit cards, cut your plastic payments in half. You don't have to pay 18 percent or more when banks offer "transfer balance" programs with interest rates of less than 10 percent for the first year. The new card issuer will help you transfer your old balance to the new card. During the next year the typical family could save almost $500 and have a year to work toward paying off the credit card debt.

Two good sources to help you find the best credit cards are the nonprofit Bankcard Holders of America (BHA). They will send you a list of low-rate and no-fee cards for $4. Write them at BHA, 524 Branch Drive, Salem, VA 24153. Another great source of helpful advice I use is RAM Research Group, a company that tracks more than 1,000 credit cards. You can call their consumer information line at 800-344-7714 and find out how to order their $5 monthly newsletter, *CardTrak,* which includes hundreds of no-fee, low-rate, and secured credit cards, and you can check out their web site:

http://www.cardtrak.com

Shop for bargains. Never give up shopping, but don't buy on price alone. The few dollars you save can cost you a lot more in the long run when the purchase falls apart. When you shop, outfits like K-Mart and Wal-Mart operate on price alone. If you buy something from a discount store, it's best to buy a major advertised brand so you can go back to the manufacturer if the product breaks down.

For example, if you want an 18-speed mountain bicycle, talk to a pro who knows bikes and learn how to fasten jugs of go-juice and what's important to look for in a new model. Then set quality standards from which you won't budge. Now, only price matters.

How much you save when you shop usually depends on how much time you spend looking for a bargain. The department stores lay it on the counter and you pay the high retail markup. But, if you want designer labels, stores like T. J. Maxx, Marshall's, Ross, and Loehman's sell the same kind of clothes you'll find in upscale shops and department stores at bargain prices.

Another suggestion is try to buy what you want wholesale. One of my favorite books on shopping is *The Wholesale-By-Mail Catalog.* For the past 19 years, each new edition tells consumers how to shop by mail, phone, or online services and save 30 to 60 percent off list prices. With more than 500 companies to choose from, the book has been featured in *Good Housekeeping* and is available in bookstores. It is published by HarperPerennial.

Another favorite shopping book is *Buying Retail is Stupid: The National Discount Guide to Buying Everything at Up to 80 Percent Off Retail.* This is a one-stop encyclopedia of discount shopping, with tips on factory-outlet malls, discount mail order, and smart shopping strategies. You can find this book in bookstores, and it is published by Contemporary Books.

Always try to buy out of season. Buy a ski parka or boots at the end of the season, or an air conditioner when it's cold outside. Have your new roof put on in the summer when it's not raining, and buy a new heater in the middle of August. The smart shopper knows that sales frequently occur when business is slow. Therefore, try to buy big-ticket items during end-of-season promotions, when merchants slash prices as much as 50 percent to clear out their inventory and keep their cash registers ringing.

Offer to buy the floor model or a recently discontinued item with full factory warranty. Chances are you can't tell the difference between the absolutely new TV, stereo, or VCR and last year's model, and floor close-outs typically sell for up to 30 percent off the price of new items.

Never buy a new car. Never drive a new car off the showroom floor. With the boom in auto leasing, late-model, low-mileage, one-owner used cars have flooded the market. The best time to buy is when the models change in September and October and leased cars are filling up the dealers' parking lots. But any time is a good time to buy because late-model used cars are always on the dealer's lot.

A good way to stretch your dollars is to buy a little-used two-year-old car with about 25,000 miles and the balance of the factory warranty from the dealer who sold or leased the car new. The biggest problem most people have with a used-car purchase is the thought that they are buying someone else's problem. But buying a used car is no longer like a trip to a casino with a cold poker hand. General Motors, Chrysler, Ford, and some imports now offer used-car warranties. And once you've selected the car, the dealer can arrange a car loan or lease you the car. I've done this for years and I'm tickled pink with all the extra options I have that I would never have paid for in the first place.

Your next new-car purchase could also kill your retirement planning. By letting someone else own the car for the first two years, when many new cars can lose as much as 40 percent of their value, the average new-car sticker price of about $21,000 should cost you used about $12,000. If you put the $8,000 you saved into a retirement plan, invested in good stock mutual funds, you might have about $125,000 in just 20 years. Then, as you race toward retirement, you can pay cash for the almost-new used car you buy and let the bankers make money on someone else.

Never forget college financial aid. When people save for college expenses, they often forget the basics. Most (94 percent) of the money for college expenses comes from the federal government, state governments, and from colleges themselves in the form of financial aid and loans. And any benefits from financial aid are also tax-advantaged. To equal each dollar your student receives, you'd have to earn 100 percent plus your tax bracket.

Here's a checklist for financial aid:

- When your student is a senior in high school, request a Free Application for Federal Student Aid (FAFSA) form. You can get general federal student aid information and the form by calling 800-4-FED-AID. Then contact each of the colleges your student is considering for its financial aid package.

- Then do a "Student Needs Analysis." This "needs" formula calculates your student's need for financial assistance by computing the parents' income and assets as well as the student's income and assets. A family of four with a $66,000 adjusted gross income (AGI) and one college-bound student applying to a $10,000-a-year college might typically start out with a "need" of $641. The difference between that figure and the college cost requires a family contribution of $9,359 ($8,484 from the parents and $875 from the student). Looking at these numbers, the first question you may ask is: "How fast can we increase our need?"

- Start planning when your student is in the ninth grade. Your IRS 1040 return that will be requested by a college will be the return for the year your student is halfway between the 11th and 12th grades. The later you understand this aspect of the aid process, the less time you have to make changes to affect your "need" numbers.

- Don't put your savings in the child's name. All the money in the student's name must be accounted for, even if it's a joint account. Each year, 35 percent of the student's money will be allocated toward paying for college costs, until the money is completely used up. If you want to exclude that money from your "needs" calculations, you must dispose of it before you sign the financial aid application. You can use the student's money for necessary college expenses, such as linens, a stereo, clothing, or your student can purchase other assets not reported on the financial aid application.

- Find a second student in your home. If a second person in your household attends college part-time (at least six credit hours), even for only one semester per year, you may qualify for a "two in college" need-increase.

- Don't hesitate to apply to expensive private colleges. Statistics show that private colleges cost approximately $5,000 to $10,000 more each school year than good state colleges and universities, but students spend on average only $1,500 more. The more expensive colleges help provide a greater "need" and typically have more money to give to their students due to alumni donations and fund-raising efforts.

The best book I've found for understanding college financial aid and student loans is *The Student Guide*. Published by the U.S. Department of Education, it explains in simple English how to apply and qualify for student aid, Pell Grants and Stafford Loans. For a free copy, write to Federal

Aid Information Center, P.O. Box 84, Washington, DC 20044-0084. The *Guide* is also available on the Web:

http://www.ed.gov

To scoop up some of the estimated billion dollars of scholarships awarded each year check out the FinAid Web site on the Internet, which links 42 different scholarship databases:

http://www.finaid.org

I also suggest *The Scholarship Book,* by Daniel J. Cassidy and published by Prentice Hall. The book covers hundreds of scholarships and how to find them. It should be in your bookstore at $24.95, or you can call 800-947-7700.

Take your lunch to work. Little things make big things happen. If you're saving for a new home or a college educa-tion, the $6 lunch you buy at work each day rather than mak-ing it at home can cost you about $100 a month, or $1,200 a year. That may not sound like much as you race around in the morning to make the sandwiches, but over just five years, the stock market has a history of turning that lunchtime savings into more than $8,000 and in ten years to about $25,000.

Use a consolidator for travel. When I travel, I book a hotel room from a hotel consolidator. These firms buy blocks of rooms at hotels in major cities at bargain prices, routinely 50 percent or more off rack rates, because hotels fear the rooms might otherwise go unsold. These firms aren't widely advertised because the hotels want you to walk up to the front desk and pay the regular rate. The ones I use are Hotel

Reservations Network (800-964-6835), Express Hotels Reservations (800-356-1123), and Quickbook (800-789-9887).

Cruise consolidators can also save you a lot of money if you can travel on short notice, usually within one or two months prior to departure. These firms tend to be low-fee membership originations. Once a member, you can call a special hotline number or look over their newsletter and find out what is currently available and save as much as 50 percent off the regular rate. The major cruise and holiday consolidators are Vacations to Go (800-338-4962) and Moment's Notice Travel Club (718-234-6295). If you want something different, Freighter World Cruises (800-531-7774) offers bargains on offbeat vacations on freighters.

LESSON 36
Putting the Pieces Together
Eight Basic Steps

A lot of people I talk with make financial planning and investing too complicated, but it's easy to see why. They are bombarded by brokers, newspaper and magazine advertisements, and investment gurus who offer the latest sure-fire undiscovered stock, or a way to double their earnings in some remote corner of the earth, or the impossible dream of high returns with low risk.

One of the most common questions I get from people worried about getting through life with an almost-empty nest egg goes something like this: "I'd like to start investing, but everything is so confusing and I don't know what to do." The good news is that you don't have to become a rocket scientist; just learning the basics will do. And, until you learn the basics, there's no need to rush into what any financial planner or broker may tell you about the best place for your hard-earned money. The advice I've given many people, who are unsure of what to do, is to simply put their money in insured CDs and give themselves time to think about where they want to invest.

"The good news is that you don't have to become a rocket scientist; just learning the basics will do."

As I ponder this lesson, I remember the many times I've taken a closer look at someone's financial situation and found that they are not ready to make investments. Instead, they have become financially bogged down because they continue to make the most common personal finance mistakes: paying too much interest, failing to set up a tax-deductible retirement plan, failing to buy enough life and disability insurance, and passing up opportunities to save money.

But life needn't be that complicated. Having read this book this far, you are now ready for my three basic elements of financial success:

1. *Priority.* Put yourself first and pay yourself first. Pay off consumer debt so you can begin to build up your savings and create a firm financial base.

2. *Time.* Extend your time horizon and look at your financial planning as a long-term job. The money you invest today will work for you for the rest of your life, both before and after retirement. The turtle may move slowly, but it always gets where it's going with steady progress, and so can you.

3. *Perseverance.* Start an investment plan and then stick to it. Month in and month out, ignore the financial news and continue to follow your plan. Maybe you can use automatic payroll or checking account deductions, you can send yourself a bill and pay your investment account each month along with the other bills, or you can use dollar-cost-averaging to add a regular amount to your investments each month.

Here are my eight basic steps you need to take, in order of priority, to build your financial security:

Step 1: Establish a budget. You won't know what you can save until you know what you must spend. Once you know what you must spend on the basics each month, find out what you can save. It's no secret that financial planning can be summed up in this simple statement: Spend less than you earn.

Step 2: Pay yourself first. Once you've established a workable budget, you can begin to pay yourself first before you pay anyone else. Don't even think about the money that has already come off the top of your paycheck. You may have a smaller amount left to manage, but you'll have much greater motivation to manage it wisely and make it stretch to cover your basic needs. Remember, if you think you're going to save what's left at the end of the month, rather than paying yourself first, you just threw a bucket of cold water on your plans to build a realistic financial nest egg.

Step 3: Pay off your personal debts. Does your credit card pop out of your wallet as if it were attracted by a magnet when you approach a shopping center? Does your monthly statement look as if you've been on a spending spree through Monte Carlo? Do you find it impossible to pay off your credit card balances in full each month? These are clear signals that you're overspending and very little of the money you earn today will be left when you need to retire or face an emergency.

Step 4: Be willing to accept some risk. No matter where you invest your money, you take a risk. In guaranteed savings, with minimal returns, you risk earning less than inflation. In higher-yielding bonds, you risk a loss of principal when you withdraw your money; and over the short-term in stocks, you risk a falling market. But risk is different than volatility. Risk is the possible loss of principal. Volatility is the possible change in the market value of an investment. For example, $1,000 in a federally insured certificate of deposit has neither risk nor volatility. Thanks to FDIC insurance, there is no risk of loss of principal. There is also no volatility because the investment is always worth $1,000.

Investing in mutual funds, however, has a risk of principal, if you withdraw your money within a few years during a down market. Mutual funds also have volatility because the market price of your investment changes from day to day. So why would anyone accept risk and volatility when they can avoid both? Because when you put your money into a fixed savings account, you pay for this lack of risk and volatility by giving up any opportunity for appreciation on your investment.

The good news is that retirement investing is a long-term project and you can overlook both risk and volatility. During this period of investing you may have some losses from time to time, but the long-term growth of equity funds has always overcome these short-term setbacks and built wealth for patient investors.

A caller on the radio asked me, "Now that I've invested in good quality mutual funds, what should I do?"

"Think of your investment in good mutual funds as bricks in a bag that you toss into the river," I said. "Once a year, check up on the contents of the bag and then come back in ten years and pull the bag up. For the most part, you cannot only forget about what's been happening to your bag of money over this period, but you'll be surprised how big it has grown when you yank it out of the river."

Step 5: Keep yourself liquid. No matter how long you plan to sock away money, life has a habit of creating change. You may become ill, your son or daughter may decide at the last minute to go to college, you may lose your job, you may have a chance for that once-in-a-lifetime vacation and that's not a good time to find out you can't touch your money.

Most of what I invest in is liquid and I know in advance—before I invest—what it will cost me to grab my money in a hurry. My bank will always cash in my CD, my bond and stock mutual funds stand ready to buy my shares anytime I want to sell, and my real estate is liquid with mutual funds that invest in Real Estate Investment Trusts. If you've ever talked with someone who needed their money and couldn't get it, these words should be chiseled into your mind as you plan your financial future.

Step 6: Buy adequate insurance. Your next priority in building financial security is to protect yourself and your family from loss. Even though life and disability insurance are very inexpensive, most of the people I talk with at my investment seminars want to *invest* for the future before they *protect* the future. Planning for the unexpected is as important as planning for the future because without adequate insurance your financial security can crumble and leave you and your family on food stamps.

Step 7: Take advantage of your employer's retirement plan. Think of your employer's retirement plan as a forced way to save and delay taxes. Regardless of what tax-deferred plan you have, start contributing now. It will require a small sacrifice each month by payroll deduction, but with the magic of compounding, you can build financial security while others are maxing out on credit cards and waiting for government handouts.

Step 8: Safeguard the money you already have. Unlike our parents' era, when the breadwinner was likely to stay with a company for 30 years and retire on a company-paid pension and a gold watch, this generation of workers will change jobs as many as six or eight times and lose much of its future retirement benefits along the way. These turbulent times aren't for the meek, and they are not for the average worker who squanders future retirement assets with each job change.

The best advice I can give you is to learn everything you can about your employer-sponsored retirement plan and how, with each job change, you can save as much of the money you and your employer have contributed to your retirement plan. While the amount you save with each job change may be small, the amount it builds to at retirement can be huge and make the difference between vacations in Europe and working behind a fast-food counter.

The point of this lesson is to ask you to change your lifestyle and incorporate my eight steps to financial security in your financial planning. Once you've set them in motion, you'll find they are easy to accomplish and well within your means.

After all, as I say over the radio, becoming wealthy today is easy if you follow a plan and regularly invest a portion of your hard-earned money.

Here again are my eight basic steps to build your nest egg:

1. Establish a budget.
2. Pay yourself first.
3. Pay off your personal debts.
4. Be willing to accept some risk.

5. Keep yourself liquid.
6. Buy adequate life and disability insurance.
7. Take full advantage of retirement plan opportunities.
8. Safeguard the money you already have.

In closing, let me tell you why I believe most people fail to build a sizable nest egg for retirement. They don't understand that even though they can only save a small amount to invest each month, if they invest that money regularly they should make, by the time they retire, 80 to 90 percent more than they invested.

Most investors also don't realize that the best chance they may have of building wealth will probably not come from following the advice of financial gurus or professional investment advisers, but from their own knowledge, intuition, and from understanding the risks they are comfortable with. If you trust what you've learned about financial planning and rely on your own instincts, the chances are that you'll build the wealth you seek.

The good news is that in spite of what you may think, the basic rules for financial success have not changed. But they work only if you put them to work and follow my eight basic steps, and most important of all, make up your mind that you want to become rich. I hope you find your dream of financial independence. I know you have the opportunity to do so.

INDEX

Total return, 78–80
Travel, saving on, 167–68
Two-cycle balance method, 17

U–V

U.S. Treasury bills, 11
USA Today, 9–10, 150
Used-car warranties, 164
Vanguard Funds, 109
Vesting, 122–26
    gradual and instant, 124–25
Volatility, 171

W

Wedbush Morgan Securities, 153
Wells Fargo Bank, 63
Wholesale-By-Mail Catalog,
    162–63
*Why You Should Select a Fee-Only
    Planner,* 158
Wollin, Gary, 153